Popular Mechanics

do-it-yourself encyclopedia

The complete, illustrated home reference guide from the world's most authoritative source for today's how-to-do-it information.

Volume 4

BODY CARE AND CAR APPEARANCE

to

CAMERAS

HEARST DIRECT BOOKS

NEW YORK

Acknowledgements

The Popular Mechanics Encyclopedia is published with the consent and cooperation of POPULAR MECHANICS Magazine.

For POPULAR MECHANICS Magazine:

Editor-in-Chief: *Joe Oldham*
Managing Editor: *Bill Hartford*
Special Features Editor: *Sheldon M. Gallager*
Automotive Editor: *Wade A. Hoyt, SAE*
Home and Shop Editor: *Steve Willson*
Electronics Editor: *Stephen A. Booth*
Boating, Outdoors and Travel Editor: *Timothy H. Cole*
Science Editor: *Dennis Eskow*

Popular Mechanics Encyclopedia

Project Director: *Boyd Griffin*
Manufacturing: *Ron Schoenfeld*
Assistant Editors: *Cynthia W. Lockhart*
  Peter McCann, Rosanna Petruccio
Production Coordinator: *Peter McCann*

The staff of Popular Mechanics Encyclopedia is grateful to the following individuals and organizations:

Editor: *C. Edward Cavert*
Editor Emeritus: *Clifford B. Hicks*
Production: *Layla Productions*
Production Director: *Lori Stein*
Book Design: *The Bentwood Studio*
Art Director: *Jos. Trautwein*
Design Consultant: *Suzanne Bennett & Associates*
Illustrations: *AP Graphics, Evelyne Johnson Associates, Popular Mechanics Magazine, Vantage Art.*

Contributing Writers: Pack Bryan, *Keep your windshield clean*, page 404; John Capotosto, *Colonial bookstand*, page 432; Rosario Capotosto, *Bookends personalized for you*, page 424; *Book-go-round for your desk*, page 428; *Cookbook caddy*, page 433; Virginia Demoss, *Bottling houses*, page 437; Phil Geraci, *Keep your camera shooting with these simple checks*, page 507; Bob Grewell *Telephoto gunstock that's inexpensive to build*, page 510; Bill Hartford, *Redecorate with a bookcase wall*, page 413; Len Hilts, *Used camera buying tips*, page 503; Paul Levine, *Cabinets to make a room*, page 475; Wayne C. Leckey, *Build an inside-the-wall bookcase*, page 418; *From bottles to fancy glassware*, page 434; *Colonial cupboard for your china*, page 487; *Space adders for crowded kitchens*, page 496; Mike McClintock, *Butcher block furniture*, page 465; David L. Miller, *Cameras—an introduction*, page 498; Mort Schultz, *Dents: how to get rid of them*, page 392; Richard Sickler, *Colonial bookrack*, page 430; David Warren, *Bookcase designs*, page 409; *Book shelves of all kinds*, page 421; *Cabinets: a place for everything*, page 469; Steven Willson and Steve Fay, *Multipurpose wall cabinets*, page 480; Ralph S. Wilkes, *Colonial pie safe*, page 483.

Picture Credits: Popular Mechanics Encyclopedia is grateful to the following for permission to reprint their photographs: Canon U.S.A., Incorporated, page 500 (top right); Eastman Kodak Company, page 499 (top and center); Konica U.S.A., Incorporated, page 501 (bottom right); E. Leitz, Incorporated, page 500 (left); Library of Congress, page 498; Ricoh Corporation, page 501 (top right); Rolleiflex—Rolleli, a division of Berkey; Marketing Companies, page 502; Charles Self photo, page 499.

ISBN 0-87851-157-1

Library of Congress 85-81760

10 9 8 7 6 5 4 3 2 1
PRINTED IN THE UNITED STATES OF AMERICA

Although every effort has been made to ensure the accuracy and completeness of the information in this book, Hearst Direct Books makes no guarantees, stated or implied, nor will they be liable in the event of misinterpretation or human error made by the reader, or for any typographical errors that may appear. WORK SAFELY WITH HAND TOOLS. WEAR SAFETY GOGGLES. READ MANUFACTURER'S INSTRUCTIONS AND WARNINGS FOR ALL PRODUCTS.

Contents

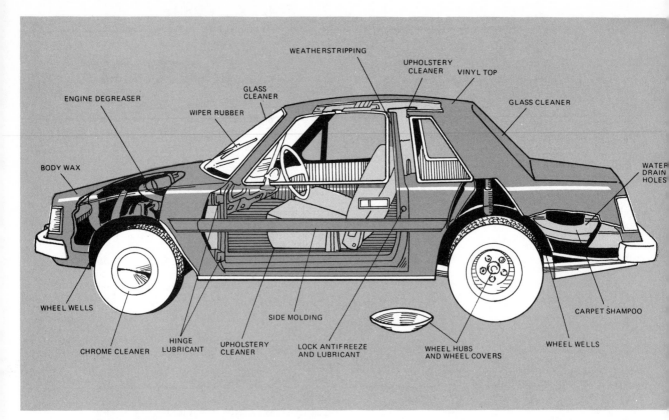

Car care inside and out

■ NOISE, RADIOS, body leaks, paint and finish are the problems most owners have with their auto bodies. Each of these areas can be of major concern to an owner who annually puts many miles on his car.

Some cars have annoying rattles from day one. Nobody seems to be able to pinpoint the exact location of some rattles. Finding the source may be one of the toughest tasks you face. Fixing the rattle, squeak, groan, whistle or whatever is usually simple.

Drive the car on different road surfaces, over bumps and at different speeds to establish whether noise is coming from the body or chassis. Once you have settled on the body (you've ruled

out such chassis areas as the engine, suspension and exhaust), establish if noise is being caused by loose body bolts (nonunitized body), broken weld (unitized body), or a loose door or window.

Tracking down body noise

If the car has a nonunitized (or partially nonunitized) body, loose body bolts will cause rattles that are more pronounced when the car goes over bumps. Tighten bolts with a torque wrench to manufacturer specifications, which is usually 25 to 30 ft.-lb.

If the car has a unitized (or partially unitized) body, a weld that has broken loose will produce a groan or squeak that's amplified when the car goes over bumps. The broken weld should be found and repaired by a repair shop that has a spot-welding facility.

Most times body noise is produced by something that's come loose. To find the rattle, start at one end of the car and gently tap every spot from top to bottom with a rubber mallet. Take your time and tap every inch of the fenders, doors, hood, trunk lid and windows.

When you hear a rattle, stop and tighten bolts in the area. Test again. If a part is held by a catch or rides on hinges, lubricate the catch or hinge and test again.

If you hear a rattle when striking the center of a door, there might be something lying inside the door—maybe a bolt that's dropped from place or even a tool left in the door during assembly. Remove the trim panel and investigate.

Rattles from a window are caused when channel weatherstripping comes loose or wears out, or a window regulator goes bad.

There's another possibility that exists when a door rattles: The door may not be aligned correctly. One way to find out is to look at the gap between the door and the adjacent fender. Now check the gap between the door and fender on the other side of the car. If there's an appreciable difference between the two gaps, it indicates that the rattling door should be realigned. Here's how:

● Loosen door hinge bolts.

● Using a pry bar, move the door until the gap between the door and adjacent fender is equal to the gap between the door and adjacent fender on the opposite side of the car.

● Tighten hinge bolts securely.

● Realign the door striker plate by loosening striker plate bolts and taking the plate off. Insert (or remove) metal striker plate shims behind the plate until a clearance of ³⁄₃₂ to ⁵⁄₃₂ inch between striker plate and door lock is obtained. Shims may be purchased from an auto supply and accessory dealer, or from the parts department of a dealer selling your make car.

To get a clear shot at measuring that distance between the striker plate and door lock, clean off both parts and apply a layer of grease or graphite to the striker plate bolt. Open and close the door once or twice. A pattern from the door lock will impress itself on the grease or graphite. Measure from the pattern to the tip of the striker plate bolt to establish the clearance between striker plate and door lock (remember, it should be ³⁄₃₂ to ⁵⁄₃₂ inch). Excessive distance between the two components causes a door to rattle. Insufficient clearance interferes with locking action.

Tracking down chassis noise

Suppose during your road test you determined that noise was coming from a chassis part rather than the body. Chassis parts that produce noise most often are the alternator when it comes loose on its mounting bracket; power steering and air-conditioner mounting brackets; motor mounts; suspension·parts, such as loose shock absorbers and sway bars; and exhaust system components.

Each should be inspected closely. The toughest noise to find is one produced in the engine compartment. A handy tool you may want to consider buying to help you isolate noise is an auto

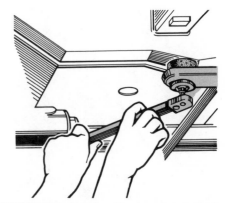

TIGHTENING body bolts with a torque wrench may eliminate an elusive rattle.

stethoscope. When placed against a part, it amplifies any noise the part may be producing, leaving no doubt about the noise source.

Tracking down radio problems

"Cutting in and out" is defined as a radio that is playing normally and suddenly dies—and then comes back on. Don't confuse it with station fade which occurs when you drive away from an area served by a particular station.

Cutting in and out is caused by loose connections or by wires that ground themselves out as you drive along.

Connections to the radio's ground, and connections to the battery, antenna and remote speakers (if any) should be tightened and inspected for integrity. Broken wires should be replaced or spliced together.

Incidentally, if the radio is dead (dial light out) don't rush to have a radio repairman pull it from the car—not before you replace the fuse serving the radio in the car's fuse block and try the radio.

Interference is normally produced by the car's ignition system. Every car with a radio has a means of suppressing this interference. Some have RF (radio interference) shields in the distributor; some have resistor wires as part of the ignition wiring; still others call for using resistor-type sparkplugs. Resistor wiring is the method that goes awry most often. When it happens, replacing the resistor wire is in order, or you can always use resistor-type sparkplugs.

By the way, if you have a stereo tape player in your car, don't forget to clean the player's head periodically—every 100 hours of operation is the recommended interval. Follow cleaning instructions in the owner's manual. Normally all that is required is cleaning the player head with a cotton swab that's been dipped in alcohol.

REALIGNING a car door requires an adjustment to door striker plate.

Important: Never apply any lubricant to a stereo tape player, and don't bring any magnetized tools near the head. If the head becomes magnetized, every tape you insert into the player will be ruined.

Stopping body leaks

The procedure to follow if water is leaking into the car's interior is: 1. find the source of entry; 2. seal it up.

To find a water leak, the first thing to do is tape a garden hose minus its nozzle to the roof of the car. Put a tin can right ahead of the spout so water coming from the hose overspreads the entire windshield or rear window.

If the leak has been showing up in the front of the car, test the windshield. Chances are the opening is there. If the leak has been showing up in back, water down the rear window. Be sure the entire expanse is covered with water. Then get inside the car and wait to see where the water starts leaking in.

Have patience. A leak may not show up for a while.

Very important: Every 5 or 10 minutes, get out of the car and rock it from side-to-side. This action allows water which is leaking through the windshield and collecting in a seam to untrap itself so it can start dripping into the car's interior.

When you establish without doubt where water is leaking into the car during this test, you should apply windshield sealer around the glass.

But this is important: Do *not* apply windshield sealer over chrome molding strips. You won't seal the leak, but instead you will "seal" the molding in place. This means that when you finally remove molding to make the repair prop-erly you will have to exert extraordinary pressure behind the strips to pop them loose. This pressure will probably be strong enough to crack the expensive windshield.

To correctly seal a leak through a windshield, remove chrome molding with a professional-style windshield molding removal tool, which may be obtained from an auto parts and accessories dealer, or from an auto body repair shop.

Slide the tool under the molding until it hits a clip holding the chrome in place. Twist the tool gently until the molding pops loose from the clip. As you get to each clip, mark its location with chalk to facilitate replacement.

Never try removing molding strips with a screwdriver or pry bar. You will crack the glass.

After all strips have been removed, take one of the holding clips to an auto body shop or auto supply and accessories store and get a number of new clips. You should not reuse the old ones, which will become distorted when you remove the molding.

Place a new clip in each spot where an old clip had been. Then apply a generous bead of auto windshield sealer as directed on the package. Make certain that every inch of the perimeter is covered with sealer. Leaving a bare spot offers a gap through which water may enter.

After applying windshield sealer, reinstall molding. Place the strips over the edges of the glass and pop them back on the clips.

Other areas of leakage

Water can leak through windows, doors, windshield wiper bosses, holes in the firewall, drip rails over doors, and fender joints.

Play a heavy stream of water from a hose on every cranny and crack as someone in the car keeps his eyes peeled. If water leaks into the car, seal the particular spot being doused. If water is entering the car through a window or door, the weatherstripping is either loose or worn. Fix or replace it.

Getting rid of body rust

There are four methods to remove rust spots:

1. Grind the spot down and/or cut away rusted metal as necessary. Back up the repair with the screening material included with the body-repair kit you're using, and apply body filler. Sand and paint.

2. Grind the spot down, making sure you get rid of all loose, rusted metal, and cover the area with aluminum tape, which comes in four-inch-wide strips. See that the tape extends at least one inch beyond the damage and adheres tightly at all of the edges.

Roughen up the tape with 100-grit sandpaper, apply plastic body filler, shape and sand, then paint.

3. Grind the damaged area and attach a piece of 20 to 22-gauge sheet metal with a riveting tool. Roughen the metal, apply plastic filler, shape and sand, then paint. Pay particular attention to edges. Make sure body filler is feathered into the car's body so edges are sealed.

4. Weld or braze sheet metal to the car's body. This is the permanent way of making the repair.

Minimizing paint problems

Today's car finishes are better than ever, so there's no reason why the paint on your car shouldn't sparkle for the life of the vehicle. The easiest and least expensive way to preserve the original luster is to wash the car as often as you can. Washing gets rid of tree sap, road tar, insects and bird droppings, gasoline, industrial fallout and other harmful agents. Always use cold water, never wash in the direct rays of the hot sun, and wait until the metal is cool. Your auto parts and accessories dealer has available car wash compounds and agents which will remove stubborn tar and other contaminants.

After washing and cleaning—and once a week isn't too often for this important car-care job—you should inspect your car's finish closely. Oxidized paint looks chalky, or gives the appearance of a film hiding the true color of your car. You'll have to use a cleaner to remove the dead paint and a wax to lay on a new protective coating—or you can use a combination cleaner/wax that will do the job in one step.

There is a wide range of cleaners and waxes available, including wax-impregnated cloths, sprays, liquids and presoftened pastes. You may want to stock all of these, and use whichever suits your needs at the moment, whether a spot polishing or a real elbow-grease job.

Use a circular motion when you polish. Do one section at a time, making sure to overlap sections. As you polish, the cloth will rub off dead paint, so turn the cloth frequently.

You'll know the wax is dry when it begins to haze on the surface. Using a clean cloth, remove the wax and buff to a high shine. Again, turn the cloth frequently.

Vinyl tops need their own special care. Frequent washing is as vital for a vinyl top as it is for the car's paint finish—maybe even more so. A soft-bristled brush is a help in thoroughly cleaning with mild soap. When the surface is clean and dry, you can use vinyl top dressing on the roof. You can use the neutral, or colorless, product or get the color that matches your vinyl top.

Scratches or cuts in the vinyl can also be repaired now, using one of the repair kits made for the purpose.

Important: Wood-grain appliqué should be washed only. Do not polish.

When cleaning a car, take time to spiff up the interior. Here are some tips:

● Thoroughly vacuum carpeting. If there is a soiled spot, it may be removed with carpet cleaner. Make sure carpets are dry before closing windows and doors.

● Wash bright metal parts with lukewarm water and a mild soap. Rinse. Do not use metal polishes.

● Remove dust and loose dirt that accumulate on interior seat fabrics with a vacuum cleaner or whisk broom. Soils, stains and spots can usually be cleaned away with a good-quality fabric cleaner.

● Clean seat belts with a mild soap solution and lukewarm water. See that they're not frayed—and use them.

Tips about other body areas

Here are a few other points about problem body areas that you may find valuable:

● If new windshield wipers streak, it probably means that arm tension is excessive. You may be able to relieve tension yourself by gently bending the arm, but don't go to extremes. If this doesn't work, tension should be tested with an ounce scale and reset to manufacturer requirements.

● If windshield-washer reservoir is full, but you're not getting a solid squirt of fluid, be sure the little nozzles aimed at the windshield are clear, and also see to it that the filter in the windshield washer reservoir is not clogged. You'll need a pin or small stiff wire to clean out the washer nozzles.

● Window smog is a problem in many cars having vinyl and imitation leather interiors. These plastic coverings give off an agent that coats windows. Try cleaning smog away with a good-quality windshield cleaner or a strong solution of ammonia and water.

● Hub caps that creep and make noise may be silenced by having another two or three lugs welded to them to hold them still.

● Speedometer cables seldom need greasing, but if one begins making noise you will need a service manual to find out how to remove it for lubrication.

Dents: how to get rid of them

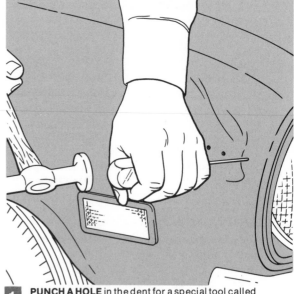

 PUNCH A HOLE in the dent for a special tool called a slide hammer. This is the way to do it if there is no other way you can get behind it to push it out.

WEAR SAFETY GOGGLES

■ CAR OWNERS CAN repair dents and rotted areas themselves. When you consider what a professional can charge for repairing a minor dent, this is good news. The tools and materials you need to repair your car's body are readily available.

The slide hammer is the best tool to straighten dents. You can buy it at most auto parts or auto body supply stores.

Begin repairs by punching holes in the dent an inch apart. Use an awl. Screw the slide hammer into a hole; it has a threaded tip. Slam the sliding arm back against the hammer's handle to straighten the dent—one blow should do. Go on to the next hole. (If the dent is shallow—a maximum of three inches in diameter and one-quarter-inch deep—it isn't really necessary to pull it out if you don't have a slide hammer.)

Bare-metal the spot. This can be done easily enough with a grinding disc that's attached to an ordinary electric drill. Grind an area which is three to four inches *beyond* the dent.

You are now ready to mix the repair material, which is plastic body filler and hardener. You can purchase the filler in gallon and quart sizes.

The filler has an indefinite shelf life as long as the lid is kept on tight and it is not mixed with the hardener. The hardener comes in a toothpaste-type tube.

It is essential that the plastic filler and hardener be properly mixed together. Follow instructions on the container. Mixing is made easier by the fact that the filler is white or gray, and the cream hardener is in a color. You are able to see when the two are thoroughly blended.

Don't mix too much. For most dents, a glob of filler no larger than the size of a golf ball and strip of hardener about one-half-inch long is sufficient. Mix them together on a clean, flat piece of cardboard or metal.

You have from 5 to 15 minutes working time after the filler and hardener are mixed, depending on the temperature. The hotter the day, the quicker the mix will set.

Avoid making repairs if the car's body is cool (under 60° F.) or damp. The filler will develop pinholes and will not set properly. The ideal working conditions are with the metal dry and temperature at 65°-75° F.

Use a body-repair-compound plastic applicator to apply body filler. Applicators are available (three to a package, each a different size).

Apply the body filler in light coats until it is built up to a height of an eighth to a quarter inch above the surface. If you have ever spackled gypsum wallboard, use the same technique. Don't lay on globs—mold on one light coat after another.

Keep the filler off paint. It doesn't stick well and could eventually crumble.

Allow the filler to set up, but this doesn't mean that it should be permitted to get solid. You don't want it hard.

The filler is ready for the next repair step when you can put a scratch in it with your fingernail without having the material come up in a glob. At the ideal working temperature, this takes 15 to 20 minutes.

Using a Surform, "mold" the filler while removing excess. Surform resembles a plane to which the blade is attached. Blades are shaped flat for flat surfaces, half-round for contoured surfaces and rattail for tight curves.

Shave off 80 to 90 percent of the built-up filler, and then let the repair set until it gets very hard. This takes at least 30 minutes.

Now, using a sanding block fitted with a piece of 40-grit sandpaper, sand the area. Follow this

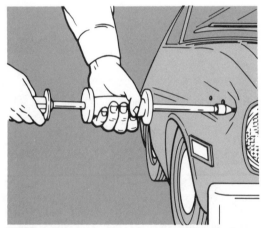

2 **THE SPECIAL** body-repair tool shown here is a slide hammer. The hammer enables you to pull out a dent after you have screwed it into a hole.

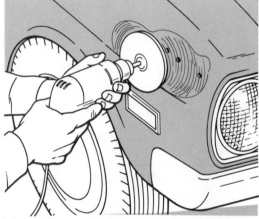

3 **GRIND THE AREA** around the dent right down to the bare metal with an electric drill.

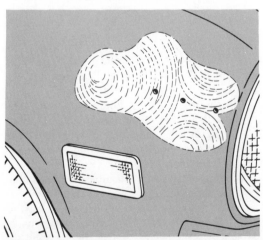

4 **MAKE IT A HABIT** always to extend the repair area several inches around a dent so that the final filling and painting can be feathered.

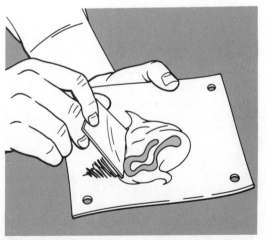

5 **ADD THE CREAM** hardener to the plastic filler, following instructions, and mix them thoroughly. The applicator comes with the filler kit.

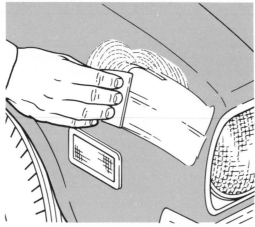

6 **PLASTIC FILLER** should be applied one layer at a time, and built up like spackling wallboard, until it is slightly higher than the body.

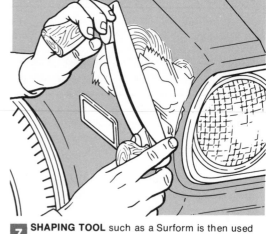

7 **SHAPING TOOL** such as a Surform is then used to remove any of the excess filler before you begin sandpapering the spot as flat as possible.

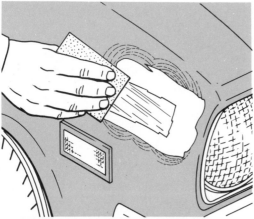

8 **TO FEATHER-EDGE** the repair, sand from the body paint area into the repair area. Be careful not to press down too hard!

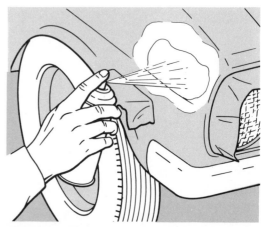

9 **APPLY PRIMER** to the repair area quickly and carefully. It's always a good idea to practice your spraying technique on a tin can first.

with a sanding using 100-grit sandpaper attached to the sanding block. Sand until the area is relatively smooth.

Avoid sanding the repair material while holding the sandpaper with your hand. You are likely to remove too much material and end up with a shallow spot.

You now need a piece of 220-grit, wet-or-dry sandpaper to feather-edge the paint around the repair area. Keep this paper wet, and sand from the paint edge into the repair area until you have a level surface. You should not feel any difference in the surface when running your hand over it.

If you are working near body trim or lights, mask them and apply a light coat of primer.

Primer is available in spray cans. If primer oversprays on to paint, you can wipe it off. You really need not mask off paint around the area until you are ready to spray paint on the repair.

Let the primer dry—about 15 minutes—and apply a light coat of auto-body glazing putty. This material fills sandpaper scratches and other imperfections. Follow application instructions on the container.

Glazing putty comes in tubes, in quart cans and in gallons. It goes on very smoothly.

Allow the work to set and dry for at least an hour. Then, using No. 320 wet-or-dry sandpaper attached to the sanding block, lightly sand the entire repair. Follow with a coat of primer. Finally, mask off the area to keep overspray from getting on body paint, and paint the spot. To get the proper color, obtain the paint code from the identification plate attached to the car's cowl or door pillar.

There is usually no problem with ordinary colors, but it may be pretty tough getting an exact match if your car is painted with a metallic paint. Paint used on imported cars is also hard to match. The equipment used at the factory, such as electrostatic paint guns, can't be duplicated by most professional auto-body repairmen, let alone laymen.

If you find it hard to match your paint color with a spray-can product, you can buy a compressed-air supply and paint separately. You can buy paint made by automotive paint manufacturers in quart or gallon size from an auto-body supply house.

The compressed-air kit is an aerosol supply to which is attached a glass or plastic container into which paint is poured.

Handling body rot

There are three ways to tackle a body rot problem. Two methods won't cost you much, but they are temporary. The third is more costly, but it is permanent. The least expensive and easiest way to do the job is with aluminum tape, which comes in four-inch-wide rolls. Break off pieces of rot and grind the area down to bare metal.

Place the tape over the rot, making sure that it extends at least one inch beyond the damage. Use 100-grit sandpaper to roughen up the tape. Then continue the repair in the way described above for repairing dents. This method will last about six months. Then the repaired area will start bubbling out.

A longer-lasting (but temporary) repair can be made with a piece of sheet metal that's the same gauge as the metal of your car (in most cases, 20 or 22-gauge). Be sure the sheet metal extends one inch beyond the rotted area. Grind the damaged spot and attach sheet metal with a Pop-rivet tool that you can buy in hardware stores.

Roughen up the sheet metal with a grinding disc, and proceed with the repair as described above. Pay close attention to applying filler between the metal and car body. Feather the filler into the body so you can't see the contour made by the patch.

Here again you are attaching one piece of metal to another. Eventually condensation and dust will get behind the repair, and it will break down. Figure on getting no more than two years.

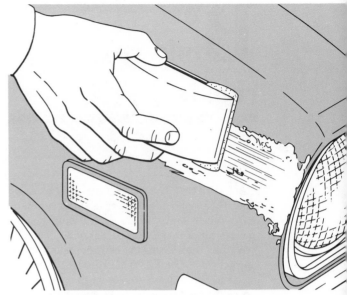

10 SAND THE REPAIR area until the plastic filler is brought down to the level of the surrounding area before you begin to feather-edge.

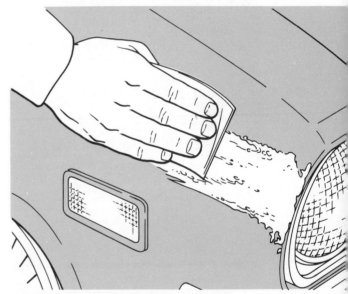

11 AUTO-BODY glazing compound is a final smoothing step. You are then ready to apply the paint to match the color of the car.

The permanent way of fixing body rot is by welding or brazing sheet metal right to the car's body. If you had a body shop do the job from start to finish, the cost might be considerable. But you can reduce it.

Have a professional do only the welding. Then, using the procedures outlined above, you finish the job.

Body rust repair

■ BODY RUST can make a car old before its time. This is particularly a problem in northern parts of the country, where ice and salt combine to rob a car of useful years of service.

Washing and waxing the body periodically will help get rid of elements that cause rust. In washing a car, play a heavy stream on the underbody, especially inside fender wells and underneath

ALUMINUM TAPE and other material make possible body repair in the home garage.

rocker panels. This will wash away road salt, a leading cause of rust.

If rust appears, it should be eliminated as soon as possible to keep it from spreading. Sand it down and touch up the spot with matching paint. In the case of extreme rust, where metal is eaten away, one of three repair methods may be employed, as follows:

1. Grind the rusted area until the rust is eliminated. Cover the spot with aluminum tape, which comes in 4-inch widths. See that the tape extends at least 1 inch beyond the damage and that edges of the tape adhere to the body.

Using a piece of 100-grit sandpaper, roughen the tape. Apply plastic body filler as directed in the instructions accompanying the body repair kit. Kits may be obtained at auto supply and accessories counters.

Use a Surform tool to mold the plastic body filler into shape. Then, sand the spot with 40-grit sandpaper which is held in a sanding block. Follow by sanding with a 100-grit sandpaper, again using a sanding block. Continue the sanding until the plastic material is even with the surface of the car body.

Using a piece of 220 wet-or-dry sandpaper and sanding block, feather the repaired area; that is, sand from the center of the area into the body. Keep the sandpaper wet and continue sanding until the repaired spot is just as smooth as the body. Paint the spot.

An auto supply and accessories dealer can help you match the color of the paint if you supply the correct code number. This number is included on the vehicle identification plate, which is attached to the firewall or door pillar.

This repair can be done by the home mechanic. It is effective, but not as long lasting as the other two methods.

2. Get a piece of sheet metal that is of the same gauge as the metal of the body (usually 20 or 22-gauge). This piece should be large enough to extend 1 inch beyond the rust area.

Grind the rust area until rust is eliminated. Attach the piece of sheet metal to the body. This can be done with Pop rivets.

Roughen the sheet metal with a grinding disc. Then, use a plastic filler kit and paint to complete the repair. When applying the plastic repair material, pay careful attention to the edges of the sheet. Use enough filler and feather it into the body. Otherwise the lines of the sheet metal will show.

Most home mechanics are capable of performing this repair, which is more effective than applying aluminum tape, but less effective than the third method.

3. Have a piece of sheet metal welded over the area after grinding off rust. The metal should be the same gauge as the body. A machine shop or auto body shop can do this for you.

With the metal in place, complete the repair yourself using a plastic filler kit and paint.

Use touch-up paint to cover any nicks as soon as you spot them, and keep a good protective coating of wax on your car's body and you'll minimize the time you have to spend on body repair!

This is the only way to stay ahead of the corrosion that shortens your car's life. You've got to become a fanatic about body care! Wash your car at least once a week to get off the surface dirt that holds pollutants against the finish. When you make it a habit to keep your car free of dirt, you'll find that it's easier to detect spots of tar, bird droppings, nicks and other road crud before they get their teeth into your finish.

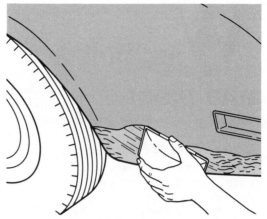

METICULOUS SANDING is critical and you should use a block to prevent raggedness.

Simply keeping your car *clean* will preserve its life, and preserve its appeal to you as the years go by. For some, washing is all the care they give the modern finishes on their automobiles. Others, however, use cleaners and waxes to take off the oxidized layer of paint, expose the car's true color and lay on a protective film that will shape those raindrops into big beautiful beads.

You've got your choice of various cleaners and waxes to do the job—from liquids, sprays and presoftened pastes to wax-impregnated cloths. Many car owners have tried all of these types at one time or another, looking for the best one to suit their needs. Many car buffs stock several different types of waxes so they can do a quick job or a real elbow-grease job depending on how much time they have.

You should polish one section at a time using a circular motion to apply the wax and making sure to overlap sufficiently. Your cloth will slowly become the color of your car as you rub off dead paint, so turn the cloth over frequently. When the wax is dry, it will haze on the surface and is then ready to be removed with a clean cloth and the surface buffed to a high shine. Again, fold the cloth frequently, as it becomes glazed with dead paint.

If you don't keep a clean machine with a regimen of "spit and polish" you'll soon find yourself driving a rust bucket.

APPLY PLASTIC body filler and use a Surform to mold materials and remove excess.

Wax, polish and paint

■ THE SHELVES OF AUTO PARTS STORES are stocked with row upon row of waxes, polishes and similar products. They fall into four main categories: straight waxes, straight cleaners (sometimes called polishes), combination cleaner/waxes and compounds.

There are two ways to restore luster to a car's finish. One is to rub out weathered paint with a cleaner or compound which brings back gloss if it's there, and then apply a coat of wax to protect that gloss. This is referred to as a two-step process. The other way is to use a single product that combines a cleaner and wax—the one-step process.

A two-step process may provide more uniform results over the long run, but it's a lot more work. Many companies sell separate waxes and polishes only because there is still a demand for them from people who prefer to do it the old-fashioned way. Most experts agree that a one-step product is just as good as a two-step.

Check paint conditions

Many people who buy new cars keep them looking good by waxing every few months with a one-step product. The silica or clay cleaning agents, although classified as "mild abrasives," do a good job of removing slightly oxidized paint called "chalk." Also contained in these products are hydrocarbon solvents (naphtha or kerosene) and detergents that will dissolve stains.

SHAPE OF WATER BEADS determines when to wax car. When tangent line of beads slumps to 50°, it's time to rewax.

But what about the older car? Can you use the easy one-step process or should you use an abrasive compound? The answer to this question lies with the condition of the paint. If it's merely dull and discolored, try a liquid cleaner. If you find yourself rubbing like crazy to make the cleaner work, move up to a paste-type compound.

About compounds

Suppose the finish looks as if it's a goner—badly weathered, stained, scratched and covered with a road film. You may think a paint job is in order, but before spending hundreds of dollars, try compounding. It just may restore the luster.

There are two types of compounds—moderate-duty (polishing compound) and heavy-duty (rubbing compound). Polishing compound, which is often white in color, removes moderately weathered paint, moderate film and light stains. Rubbing compound, usually red in color, is needed to remove badly weathered paint, heavy film and bad stains. Try a polishing compound first. If it doesn't do the job, use rubbing compound.

Put the car in a shaded area and follow the instructions printed on the compound can. Do not use a heavy hand and never use an electric buffer with rubbing compound. It is extremely abrasive and can rub off paint right down to the primer, making a new paint job unavoidable. Use light pressure and a back-and-forth motion. A circular motion leaves swirl marks on the car finish.

It will help to avoid overrubbing spots if you wash the car first and then get rid of stubborn stains like bug splatters, bird droppings, tree sap, tar and the like.

Next, wax it

After compounding the car, step back and take a critical look. If you like what you see, you've avoided the need for new paint. Then, apply wax.

Keep the vehicle out of direct sunlight, and start in the middle of a panel and work out toward the ends. Apply a little wax and use a circular, light-handed motion to spread it.

Don't assume two coats of wax are better than one. As you apply a second layer, you'll remove wax that was previously applied. Spreading on a second coat is work for nothing.

Borderline finishes

Suppose the paint on your car doesn't look all that bad. Is it advisable to use the one-step process to clean and wax at the same time? Experiment. Use a one-step product on the worst-looking area. If the results aren't good, turn to the two-step process.

ELECTRON MICROSCOPE PHOTOS show a new metallic paint job and same paint after accelerated weathering equivalent to 2–3 years in Florida. Magnification is 2000x. Wax can slow damage.

Types of one-step products

There are three general categories of one-step products: paste, liquid and spray. Results produced by paste and liquid one-step waxes are equally long-lasting, while some spray products may not be as long-lasting, since some of the active product has been given up to get more room for the fluid to permit sprayer application.

Tips about waxing

If you've ever waxed a car, you know the sides are the most difficult areas to do. You may want to tackle fenders and doors first, when you're fresh and have a full head of steam, before waxing the hood, trunk and roof.

Another trick is to know when your car needs waxing. What you do is to check how water beads on the surface. On a freshly waxed surface, beads will be almost round. As your wax protection wears down, beads will flatten out. When a line from the surface tangent to a bead gets to be 50°, it's time to wax the car again.

Besides restoring paint, here are other things you can do to make your car look sharp: Clean the engine with an engine cleaner/degreaser. Use a special cleaner to clean the wheels without marring the paint finish. A soft toothbrush is a good tool for getting into tight spots. Use chrome cleaner on bright work and a silicone-rich preservative to clean nonmetal moldings and bumper strips. Give tires a new look with tire black.

Auto body corrosion generally begins on the underside of the car where wax is never applied. Periodically hose down the underside of the car to get rid of dirt and road salt.

Understanding paint

If compounding fails to bring paint luster to an acceptable level, it's time to consider repainting. On the surface, the task looks simple enough. Just turn it over to a body shop and have it "spritzed." In reality, it is not that simple.

The price depends on the type of paint "system" used. In the economic rank order, from lowest to highest, here are the systems you'll encounter.

Baked enamel. Enamel refers to the type of binder used in the paint. Baked enamel will begin to fade after one to three years if it isn't properly cared for. It has a tendency to fade rapidly because of the sun's ultraviolet rays.

Acrylic enamel. This is the system most widely used by paint shops. The term *acrylic* refers to the type of polymer (plastic) used in the binder to hold pigment particles together. Life expectancy of acrylic colors is approximately five years, with good care. Acrylic enamel has good resistance to ultraviolet rays and fades at a minimal rate.

Acrylic lacquer. This system uses lacquer as the binder. It has been widely used by General Motors for painting new cars. It requires intense heat that is difficult for body shops to duplicate. Those body shops that can provide an acrylic lacquer paint job generally charge more for acrylic enamel.

One advantage of acrylic lacquer is that it gives a higher gloss. Its color will last about as long as acrylic enamel and has good resistance to ultraviolet rays, but it requires more frequent waxing to maintain its gloss.

Base coat/clear coat. This is the most expensive paint job you can buy. The paint is oversprayed with a super-tough urethane that protects the finish indefinitely. The urethane clear coat slows ultraviolet paint fading. If something scratches the car's surface, the urethane coat gets scratched—not the paint. Minor scratches are easily polished out. Once the clear coat is penetrated or degrades, however, the color coat fades rapidly, without the gradual dulling of traditional finishes. It is virtually impossible for the do-it-yourselfer to touch up chips and scratches on clear coat paints.

Clear coats were first introduced on imports, but they are showing up on more and more new domestic cars, too.

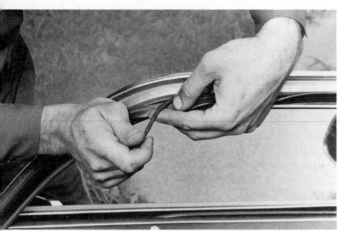

SHIM UP weatherstripping by pulling the seal away from the frame and inserting roll-type caulking.

SMALL CONSTRUCTION flaws such as solder lumps can generate annoying noise around windows.

Wind noise and water leaks repair

■ YOU NEEDN'T endure irritating wind noise while you're driving. Nor must you risk getting wet because of a hard-to-find leak—one that takes effect only when it's raining. Use the pros' techniques to find and fix these problems. It need not be difficult.

There are two kinds of wind noise: that caused by air leaks and that by turbulence.

Air leaks occur when weatherstripping around doors and windows wears out, wasn't installed properly to begin with or doesn't seal for some other reason. Turbulence—the interruption of airflow around the outside of a car—is caused by the shape of the body, or a protruding or loose part.

Tracing noise caused by leaks

You can often trace an air leak with the car parked in your driveway. Troubleshooting noise caused by turbulence usually requires a road test.

Noise caused by an air leak occurs frequently when air leaks *out of* rather than into a car, because air pressure becomes greater inside the car than outside. This happens when you drive with doors and windows closed, and air vents open, or the heater or airconditioner turned on.

Higher in-the-car air pressure forces the top edges of door glass outward. If glass loses contact with weatherstripping, the air leak that results will produce an annoying noise.

Air leaks that cause noise are normally confined to the upper part of a car to about a foot below the bottom of windows. Leaks lower down cause drafts, and may let dust and water into the car, but they seldom produce noise.

HIGH SPOTS or solder lumps can be chipped off with hammer and chisel if they're used carefully.

A HOSE USED as a stethoscope can detect air leaks when the car's interior is pressurized.

To troubleshoot a noise created by an air leak, proceed as follows:

Examine all weatherstripping for worn-out spots, tears and looseness. Reglue loose weatherstripping, using rubber cement. Worn-out weatherstripping can often be salvaged by inserting some roll-type caulking beneath the worn spot. If weatherstripping is torn or badly damaged, replace it.

Inspect each door for holes in the sheet-metal joints and for rusted-out spots. Remove rust and seal holes with auto-body caulking compound.

The bottom of each door has drain holes that allow water getting inside the door to run out. This prevents rusting. Door drain holes must *not* be sealed. In fact, you should make sure they are free. Use an awl, icepick or some such tool to clean them out.

Examine door-opening surfaces for solder lumps and other uneven spots that are preventing full contact of weatherstripping with the door frame. Solder lumps should be filed off or cut off with a hammer and metal chisel. Weatherstripping must have an even surface against which to seat firmly if air leaks and the noise they produce are to be prevented.

The least irregularity could have produced an air leak, yet escaped detection thus far. So roll up all windows and shut fresh-air inlets. The inside of the car must be completely closed off.

Start the engine and set heater or air-conditioner controls to admit air into the car. Set the blower at top speed.

Get out of the car. Check that doors and windows are tightly shut, and allow pressure to build up inside several minutes.

Take a length of hose, hold one end to your ear and pass the other end slowly around the edges of the doors and glass. Even the hiss of a small air leak will be audible.

The hose method of finding a leak is almost as reliable as modern electronic air-leak detectors used by some auto body and glass shops. The usual version has two components.

One is a signal generator that is placed inside the closed car. The other is a detecting unit held outside the car to pick up the generated tone signal. The signal can't be heard unless it is "leaking" from the car.

If you took your car to a shop that uses an electronic leak detector, the manager might not charge you for finding the leak. However, he would expect to make repairs, and they aren't free. Managers of other shops tell us that they do make a modest charge for tracing air leaks.

Up to now, we've been dealing with noise made as air inside the car leaks out. But outside air can leak in, as well, creating noise.

To determine if a leak exists because of a bad weather seal around the door, place a strip of paper between the weatherstripping and door frame. Pull the paper out. If it comes easily, without resistance, the weatherstripping should be shimmed or replaced. Check all around every door. If weatherstripping doesn't seem worn or loose, the door may be misaligned and require

CLOSING THE DOOR on a strip of wrapping paper checks tightness of weatherstripping's grip.

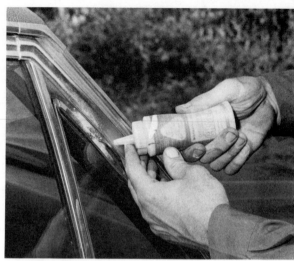

A SQUEEZE BOTTLE of marking chalk helps to check windows' seal; try to puff it through any gaps.

tightening of hinges, repositioning of the striker or some other adjustment.

Air can also leak into a car from around windows. Close each window tightly and blow tracing powder or chalk in along the edges. Check for traces of powder or chalk on the inner side of the window. If dust shows up on the inside, the window seal may have to be replaced or the window may have to be readjusted.

Tracing noise created by turbulence

You won't be able to get rid of all noise made by turbulence. There will always be some because of the design of the car.

A perfectly streamlined car wouldn't create turbulence. But it wouldn't provide much room for comfort either.

So, although some turbulence noise will be heard, you don't have to stand for noise produced by a loose or protruding part. But you have to find it. Here's how:

For your road test, select a route in an open, low-traffic area which will allow you to drive at cruising speed and to pull safely off the road to make adjustments. Equip yourself with a roll of masking tape and strips of automotive caulking. Close all windows and doors tightly. Make sure the blower is off, fresh air vents are closed, and heater and airconditioner controls are off.

Drive at the speed at which the noise annoys you. If the noise seems to be outside the car, it is being caused by turbulence. If the noise seems to

be in the car, you may have an air leak that was unnoticed during the driveway test.

Using masking tape, cover each part of the car's body that may create turbulence and noise. Molding strips are prime candidates. Cover a small section at a time. When the noise disappears during a particular phase of the road test, it means you have found the offending area.

Quite often, noise created by turbulence occurs when wind rushes under a strip of molding. This can be corrected by removing the molding strip, filling the space with automotive caulking and replacing the strip.

Another part creating noise is the weatherstrip around the outside of vent windows, especially at the lower front corner. The weatherstrip here may be distorted and pulled away from the body. Called a pucker, this could have been caused by overtravel of the vent. If weatherstrip is rubber, get rid of distortion by softening it with a heat source, such as a propane torch. When the material becomes pliable, smooth out the pucker and work the weatherstrip into shape as it cools. The distorted spot may need a few heat applications before it is finally smooth.

Another source of turbulence noise is roof railings. These, too, should be taped one small section at a time until the road test demonstrates that the noise disappears, revealing the offending section. If rails are rusted or have pulled away from the body of the car, they should be repaired if noise is to be eliminated.

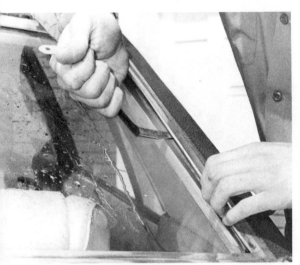

SPECIAL, LOW-COST tool helps remove windshield molding without cracking the costly glass.

RUBBER SEALING strip may pucker at the corners, causing a leak. Heat and smooth it carefully.

Tracing water leaks

There are several spots through which water can leak into a car, but the front and rear windshields are always prime candidates. Concentrate on the front one if water has appeared in the front of the car. Test the rear windshield if water has leaked into the trunk.

Tape a garden hose, minus a nozzle, to the top of the car and place a can in front of the snout. See that water spreads over the entire windshield.

Keep water flowing for at least 30 minutes; it may take this long for water to show up inside the car. Now and then, rock the car from side to side. Water occasionally accumulates in a seam along the windshield and will leak into the car only when the car corners.

Resealing a front or rear windshield is no easy task. You shouldn't apply sealing compound right over molding. It often won't provide an adequate seal, and if the windshield ever does have to be removed, you're more likely to break the glass.

Molding should come off, but don't use a screwdriver or some other common tool. You could crack the glass. Instead, get a windshield clip tool. One style is for Chryslers; another for other domestics. They're inexpensive. Slip the tool beneath the molding and slide it along until it touches each molding clip. Twist the tool to pop the molding loose from the clips.

Buy new molding clips (same kind as the old clips) from an auto glass dealer and insert them into place along the glass. Now, apply a liberal bead of windshield sealer around the entire circumference of the windshield. Reattach the molding by pressing it onto clips.

If a water leak up front isn't uncovered by hosing down the front windshield, apply a heavy flow of water from a hose (no nozzle) for several minutes on each spot up front that may be leaking. These include every bolt and seam along the firewall, drip rails, and the A-post (the part of the body on each side of the windshield).

Have someone in the car yell when water begins to leak. When this leak is revealed, seal the weak area with silicone rubber caulk.

If water is leaking into the trunk by some other way than through the rear windshield, the location of the leak can be found by having someone crawl into the compartment with a flashlight. Close the lid and play a heavy stream of water from a hose (no nozzle) along each part through which water can leak—including the trunk-lid seam, stop- and backup-light seams, and rear body seams. Be sure to concentrate a heavy flow of water on one section at a time for a long enough period. When your friend in the trunk sees water starting to drip in, he can yell or tap on the lid to tell you to open up.

A leaking trunk lid can often be repaired by prying off the gasket, repositioning it and gluing it back into place.

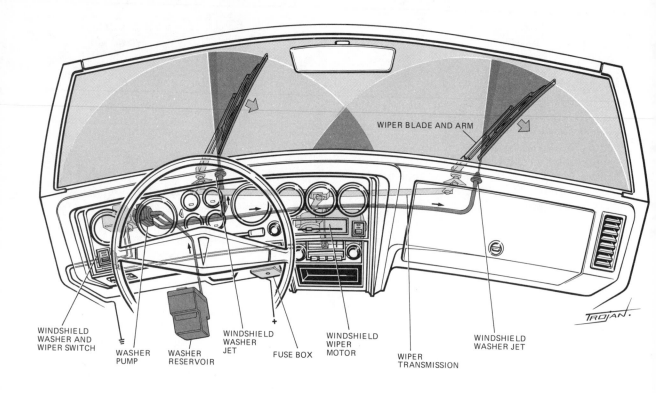

WIPER BLADE AND ARM

WINDSHIELD WASHER AND WIPER SWITCH

WASHER PUMP

WASHER RESERVOIR

WINDSHIELD WASHER JET

FUSE BOX

WINDSHIELD WIPER MOTOR

WIPER TRANSMISSION

WINDSHIELD WASHER JET

TROJAN.

Keep your windshield clean

■ IT'S A SAFE BET that, unless your car is new or you've replaced the wiper blades within the last few months, your wipers are streaking or skipping. Wipers usually don't go bad all of a sudden, so you're not likely to notice the progressive deterioration that's going on all the time.

The quickest, easiest, safest and cheapest way to keep your wipers working effectively in all kinds of weather is to install new refills every six to 12 months. You'll want to do it more often if you live in a heavily industrialized region, and may not need so many changes if you're located in a remote rural area. Air pollution, or lack of it, is the determining factor.

Most drivers go to the needless expense of buying new blades instead of refills. The blade is the whole assembly at the end of the wiper arm, and it rarely has to be replaced. The rubber that does the work is called the refill, costs only a fraction of the price of the blade and is usually all that has to be changed.

Between replacements, however, there's plenty that you can do to help the wipers do their jobs and assure clear vision in any weather. Begin by cleaning the glass inside and out at least once a week. Even if your glass looks clean as a result of frequent trips through an automatic carwash, the chances are you have a film of wax on the surface of the glass and on the blades.

Glass manufacturers recommend that you treat the windshield as you would a fine mirror, so the old trick of using a dry paper towel or cloth to clean a dirty windshield on the theory that glass is "hard" just isn't valid. Use a mild detergent and water, or a solvent that has been made specifically for cleaning glass, to "float" the dirt away. Never use an abrasive or scouring powder, and don't try any car-polish compounds.

In the summer, road tar or bugs often build up on the surface of the windshield. Use a tar remover to get rid of the tar, then follow up with a detergent to cut the residue left by the tar-and-solvent mix.

To get rid of bugs, a plastic kitchen scouring pad (not metal) works well if one of the plastic net-covered sponges made for the purpose isn't available. Another method is to place a water-soaked towel over the windshield for half an hour

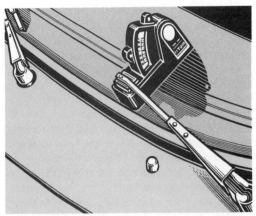

WIPER-ARM TENSION can be checked with a professional gauge. Adjust or replace; don't bend wiper arm.

WIPER PROBLEMS—WHAT TO LOOK FOR

WIPER-BLADE and wiper-arm problems are sometimes apparent, as shown in the drawings. Often, though rubber appears good, it has lost its "life." To eliminate streaking, install refills on the blades.

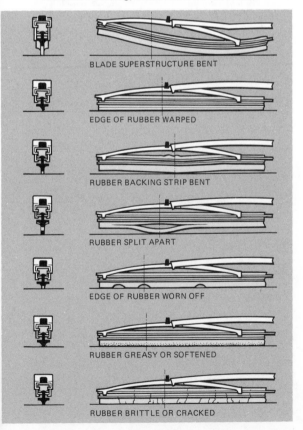

BLADE SUPERSTRUCTURE BENT

EDGE OF RUBBER WARPED

RUBBER BACKING STRIP BENT

RUBBER SPLIT APART

EDGE OF RUBBER WORN OFF

RUBBER GREASY OR SOFTENED

RUBBER BRITTLE OR CRACKED

or so. The moisture in the towel will soften the dead bugs.

Don't let grime accumulate on the inside of your windshield until it rivals waxed paper for transparency. The build-up usually occurs more rapidly in cooler weather, when the windows are closed and the defrosters force a greater volume of air across the inside of the windshield.

Winter or summer, be sure to keep the windshield washer reservoir filled. Use washer solvent, rather than plain water. It cuts through road grime better.

Never pour boiling water on a windshield to melt ice or free the wipers. Cover the windshield at night with a blanket or a sheet of plastic to keep ice from forming. When ice *does* form, be sure to use a scraper that's made for the purpose. Glass manufacturers suggest frequent examination of these scrapers for nicks that appear in the edge of the blades. Replace any damaged scrapers before they get the chance to dig into the glass.

By federal law, every car manufactured must be equipped with a windshield washer, yet it is estimated that 30 percent of the washers installed in today's cars don't work.

If yours isn't functioning, it's a fairly simple task to locate the problem. First, check to see if there's fluid in the reservoir. Then listen closely: If you hear the pump running, it's likely there's an obstruction somewhere in the line.

Remove the hose at the pump outlet and blow through it. If the fluid squirts out of the nozzles, then the filter is clogged and must be cleaned. Use a solvent to cut any oily residue that may have accumulated on the screen.

If the filter is clean, examine the hose line for

breaks, kinks or obstructions; then check the nozzles. A straight pin or sewing needle will usually clean them out. If they've corroded closed, replacement may be necessary.

If the pump itself isn't running, check all electrical connections—the switch at the dash, the fuses, and the wiring running to the pump. If you still get no action, remove the pump or the pump-wiper combination and give it a bench test just to make sure that power has been getting to the pump. Refer to your dealer shop manual for the removal procedure to avoid damage to the wiper transmission assembly.

Adjusting the washers is simply a matter of bending the nozzles a little bit at a time until you have the stream hitting the correct spot on the windshield. That spot should be about two inches below the top of the wiper arc when the car is standing still. At expressway speeds, the stream will then hit the center of the wiped area.

Rubber refill edges must be sharp enough to cut through water, but remain soft and flexible enough to maintain contact with the glass. The edges must also be perfectly straight to assure uniform pressure throughout their length. When the edges go bad, or the rubber begins to harden, the blade skids across the glass like a bald tire.

Although a blade may tear when it's yanked away from a frozen windshield, it is chemical action that causes most blade deterioration. In fact, there are indications that "exercise" through frequent use can help to extend the life of a wiper blade. In dry, hot desert country, wet the windshield with a hose and run the wipers for five minutes every few weeks. It will help keep them soft.

Arm tension

Until the early '60s, when electric wiper motors became standard, wiper-arm pressure was critical because of the low power of the vacuum motors then in use.

Today, heavy-duty electric motors permit the use of stronger springs in the arms. Average arm pressures have consequently more than doubled.

It isn't likely you'll need to test, but if you have to, here's how:

When the wiper arm is in a vertical position, remove the blade. Using a small pressure tester (most service stations will be able to find one in the back of the drawer), place the arm tip on the small platform and take your reading. If your car has a vacuum motor, the pressure should be about one ounce for each one-inch length of the blade. For an electrically powered system, pressure should be at least double that, and preferably be in the range of 32 to 36 ounces.

Removing wiper arms

Arms are easy to remove, *if you use a puller tool.* You can borrow one at your local service station, or have the dealer do the job for you. Unless you have a fleet of cars requiring constant care, there's little need to buy a tool you'll probably never need again.

Lubricating the wiper system is a matter of applying just a few drops of oil to all possible points of wear. On the wiper arm, particularly if it's a double-arm parallelogram mechanism, keep the lubrication to a minimum to avoid dripping and smearing of the glass during wiper operation. Don't forget the under-hood linkage between the motor shaft and the two arm shafts.

TYPES OF WINDSHIELD GLASS DAMAGE

STONE NICKS or chips will not spread, but replace the windshield if they're large or directly in front of the driver. Outright breakage is glass that's shattered or cracked inside or out. Replace it. Strain cracks will spread; replace windshield. Star break has cracks radiating from point of impact; damage will spread, so replace windshield. Bull's-eye half moon is a chip that's not dislodged from glass; it won't spread. Sand pits, if there are enough of them, will impair vision. Windshield should be replaced.

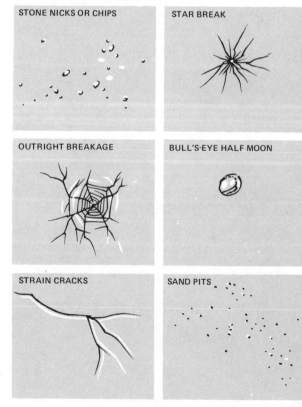

STONE NICKS OR CHIPS

STAR BREAK

OUTRIGHT BREAKAGE

BULL'S-EYE HALF MOON

STRAIN CRACKS

SAND PITS

Soundproof your car

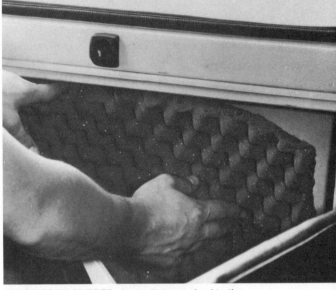

■ TODAY'S NEWER CARS have little, if any, soundproofing in the doors, hood and trunk lids. In an effort to save weight and money, sound insulation packages are reserved for the options list. In the case of low-priced, super-economy cars, soundproofing isn't even an option.

One workable solution is the installation of dense foam rubber. This is the type of foam that lines camera and electronic equipment cases. It has a curvy, hills-and-valleys configuration and comes in a variety of sheet sizes. The foam sheets come in double layers, with the hills and valleys interlocking. A 4 x 8-ft. double sheet is enough to do two entire minicars or one full-size four-door sedan.

Soundproofing the hood

You don't have to remove the hood to install the foam. It was removed here only to make photography easier.

Foam thickness varies, so you'll have to determine the clearance between the hood and the highest point of the mechanical parts under the hood. You can do this by putting a lump of clay

DENSE FOAM RUBBER sheets that are glued to the bulkheads in your car will cut down on the noise level of the vehicle. The foam should resist heat up to at least 220°F. It may be necessary to reroute wiring.

on the highest point on the engine and closing the hood. The clay will be mashed down to the thickness of the foam you need to use.

Your supplier will give you a spec sheet on the foam you buy if you ask for it. The foam used should resist temperatures up to 250°F.

Clean the inside of the hood with Trichloroethane 1,1,1 or a similar degreaser. Remove any rust or acid deposits that might have gotten on the hood from the battery. Prime the area if you scrape. If you're really fussy about appearance,

APPLY GLUE TO THE FOAM as well as to car's metal surfaces. Let the glue get tacky before installing the foam sheet.

IN AREAS HIDDEN by trim panels, expanding foam urethane provides temperature and sound insulation. Use it sparingly.

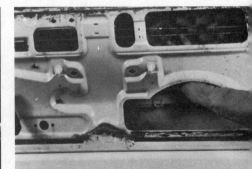

TEST-FIT THE FOAM panels and operate the lock mechanism and window winders before final gluing in doors. Be sure the foam does not interfere with any of these.

you can repaint the inside of the hood with body color paint.

Cut the foam to the approximate shape of the area to be covered. Then apply liberal amounts of silicone adhesive sealant to the metal and the foam. Wait a few minutes before bonding the foam. This lets the adhesive get slightly tacky.

After the glue has dried, use a single-edge razor to finish cutting the foam. If you have engine timing or emissions specifications labels glued to the hood, you can either try to remove them and transfer them to an inner fender, or leave a hole in the foam to keep the specs visible.

Soundproofing the trunk and door panels

You can apply the same techniques for soundproofing the trunk lid and trunk wall. The inside of door and body panels can also be soundproofed.

When you're working with a door, you need to be more careful and precise than with a hood. Be sure the foam won't interfere with lock and window-winding mechanisms.

Don't install the foam right to the bottom of the door. Leave a gap of an inch or two. If there is leakage in the future, this will allow water to drain out of the drain holes.

In rear panels with fixed glass, you can use the foam sheets coupled with an expanding foam

BEFORE INSTALLING FOAM under the hood, check for clearance with engine parts. Foam shouldn't come in contact with engine pieces. To prepare the surface for adhesive, degrease or paint as necessary.

sealant. Foam sealant does not give off any toxic fumes, which is important in a closed car; one make is fire-resistant up to 250°F. One inch has an R value of 5.

Don't be overenthusiastic about using the expanding foam sealant. Not only does it expand as it comes out of the spray can, it expands as it cures—a process that takes several hours. If you've applied too much of the foam sealant, wait until it cures and trim the excess.

BECAUSE OF RUST AND ACID deposits on the stiffening ribs, this hood needed repainting. The masked-off area, however, was still in good condition.

ROUGH-CUT THE FOAM sections and test-fit. Apply the adhesive, install and trim the foam after the adhesive has dried.

Bookcases: basic designs

■ TODAY'S BOOKCASE is often a functional, multipurpose furnishing. Books are combined with displays of art objects and family mementos. Frequently, the bookcase is an entertainment center holding not only books but the stereo system, television and video recorder.

A flexible furnishing with a history

Centuries before Johann Gutenberg printed his first book, there was a need for storage of "books." Assyrian cuneiform tablets were stacked on shelves in a great library. The scholars of Egypt had shelved walls and cabinets for the storage of parchment scrolls.

Following the invention of printing, homes of the very wealthy and cultured contained rooms with built-in shelving to hold book collections. These rooms became more and more elaborate as time passed. Shelves reached to the high ceilings and required a movable ladder to retrieve a particular volume. Some homes had mezzanines built and lined with shelves.

The free-standing bookcase, or bibliotheque, did not come into general use until the 18th century, and only then by the wealthy. Its length was greater than its height, and the front was fitted with doors, often with wire grills and lined with silk. The cabinets were built with two sections. Usually a pair of doors enclosed each of the top sections, while single doors were used on the lower sections. The elbow-height bookcase became popular in the late Georgian period, the wall space above devoted to hanging paintings.

A design for every taste

Each of us has our own individual idea of what a bookcase is. Antique lovers probably think of rich mahogany or warm-toned cherry and the splendor of framed glass doors. Those whose tastes lean to the Spartan may prefer something Shaker in design, with clean, simply stated lines. If you have school-age children, you'll doubtless consider an elaborate study center combining bookcases with drop-down desk and lots of storage space. And if you're starting out in your first

PREFINISHED SHELVING becomes an attractive instant bookcase when supported on a wall by brackets and standards. Systems like these are available at most hardware stores and home centers.

READY-TO-ASSEMBLE steel utility shelving in a variety of decorator colors is ideal for the rough-and-tumble environment of a student's room and provides support for desks and other storage areas.

home or apartment, you may regard a bookcase as prefinished shelves and brackets attached to a wall.

There is a sufficient range of bookcase designs available so you can let your imagination and creativity roam freely. Bookcases can be rigidly uniform in their shelf arrangement; shelves can be fully adjustable to fit a wide variety of book sizes; wall-hung shelves can be clustered in neat stacks or spread apart in appealing visual patterns; bookcases can fit against walls, be built into them, even serve as room-dividing walls. Styles can range from modern to cases with elegantly carved moldings. The choice is yours.

Simple bookcases

Prefinished shelving available at most hardware stores and home centers lets anyone fashion attractive book containments. Two basic types of prefinished shelves are generally stocked. One is made from particleboard with surfaces bonded with printed wood grain melamine or vinyl. These are trim in appearance, with squared corners and edges. They are rigid and resist sagging. A great variety of wood-grain patterns and solid colors is available. Shelves are supported by steel or aluminum brackets fitted to steel standards securely attached to a wall. Endless design ideas can be achieved with these systems, and changes in design can be made without relocating the wall standards.

Another type of prefinished shelf is made from pine and stained and finished in a range of light and dark tones. Usually, these are accompanied by matching wooden brackets that mount directly on a wall or hook onto steel mounting pieces. These shelf systems are not as flexible as those with brackets that attach to standards. Relocating a shelf means punching new screw or Molly-bolt holes for the brackets.

Standard bonded-finish shelf boards can quickly and easily be made into a free-standing bookcase by using specially designed brass clips. With some planning, a bookcase of almost any shape and size can be produced using nothing more than a tack hammer as a tool. The brass clips are designed for fabricating corners, joining a vertical board against a horizontal board and mating two shelves with a central vertical support.

A similar-style bookcase can be produced from decorator-colored steel utility shelves sold at hardware stores, home centers and office supply outlets. These units are ideal for the rough-and-tumble world of a teenager's room. A pliers and screwdriver are all that are required to assemble a colorful steel bookcase.

Attractive, unassembled, economical wood grain melamine-bonded free-standing bookcase wall systems are designed with special joining devices permitting assembly of a complete system using only a screwdriver.

Another and more expensive type of unassembled bookcase is available in kit form. Most parts are cut from select hardwoods, reasonably well surfaced, and ready for assembly. A few basic tools are useful, such as bar clamps to ensure tight joinery. Experience in wood finishing is also useful to satisfactorily complete a unit. But when the project is done, you have a truly fine piece of furniture.

If you have a router and sander, you can build a great-looking yet simple adjustable-shelf book-

A BOOKCASE can look like it is built into a wall when the wall is extended to surround the shelves.

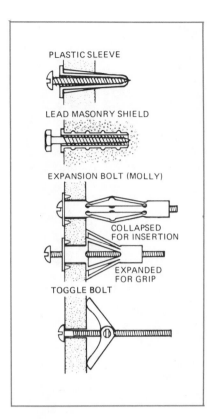

BRASS CLIPS are used to quickly assemble a bookcase with prefinished shelf boards. The clips come in three different shapes to meet every design and shelf-arrangement need.

WHEN SUPPORTING bookshelves on a wall, it is smart to use one of several types of spreading fasteners that secure tightly to a plasterboard wall. On masonry, lead or plastic sleeves can be used.

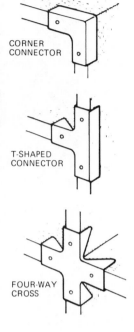

case that is precisely tailored to fit your books. Your local lumberyard will cut required hardwood boards to specified widths and lengths, so all you need to do is rout two shallow grooves in each of two uprights for recessing standards to accept shelf clips. No fancy joinery is required. Uprights lap ends at top and bottom and are glued and nailed to secure. Because the depth of the unit is relatively shallow, it is supported by a single screw at the top that is driven into a stud in the wall.

Care has to be taken when you mount bookcase standards or brackets to a wall. Molly bolts or other types of spreading fasteners should be used to give effective holding power when the support cannot be secured into a wall stud.

Sophisticated systems

If you have the tools and woodworking experience required for more sophisticated units, you can build a bookcase that serves its utilitarian purpose, but is fine-quality furniture as well. You can build a bookcase into a wall, following the directions given later in this section. The wall itself can be built out to give the bookcase the appearance of being built in. The built-in, which can have secret compartments for securing valuables, can be built against a wall or even hung on it. You can also build cabinetry that is freestanding. Cabinets can be made from rich hardwoods and veneers and stained and finished to a satin gloss. They can also be built from plywood or particleboard and painted.

Recessing a bookcase of any type into a wall has one obvious advantage: It saves some floor space that would otherwise be taken up by the cabinet. You have to be careful, however. If the wall is a structural support—that is, if it is a principal support member for the floor above or is critical to the ceiling and roof support—the project gets complicated. A jack post is needed to hold the weight while you construct a header beam to bridge the recess area. It's probably best to recess only when the bookcase is part of a new wall built in a remodeling project. Space saved is only inches, the depth of a 2x4 or less, plus the thickness of your drywall.

Space is always important, especially when you're a little cramped. Look for places where there's unused space. A great place for a bookcase for student use is inside a walk-in closet. You probably can put some of this space to work

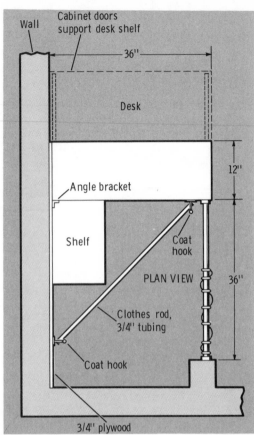

BOOKCASES CAN divide a room's space, effectively
storing books and creating more storage space.

merely by relocating a hanger bar. A floor-to-ceiling bookcase wall can hide a corner storage area.

Bookcases themselves can become fixed or movable wall units that attractively divide room space and provide storage of valued books. One application of this concept is the open see-through unit that displays both books and art ob-

jects. Augmented with a TV set, video recorder and cassette storage, a room divider bookcase becomes an entertainment center as well.

A bookcase can be almost any design, tailored to suit the specific needs, desires and woodworking experience of the individual who sets out to make it. A bookcase truly is a flexible furnishing

Redecorate with a bookcase wall

■ TURNING A WHOLE wall into a bookcase is one of those "dream" projects. You plan to do it for a long time—while books keep piling up in a corner. And if it's not books you accumulate, it's probably something else: Just about any collection can be displayed nicely on all the shelf space you get with a floor-to-ceiling bookcase. As you can see, by designing in a base row of cabinets, you also get out-of-sight storage space.

FIVE INDIVIDUALLY constructed boxes fit together to fill the living room wall. The 3-in.-wide stiles and 3⅓- in. crown molding that's continued around the room give the bookcase wall a designed-in look. The appearance and the storage space of the 12-in.-deep unit is enhanced by the row of base cabinets with raised-panel doors.

THE TOP two bookshelves are designed to be adjustable.

A HATCH built into the bottom of one or more cabinets gives you a place to hide cameras and other valuables.

Selecting the right location

Usually, the wall selects itself. It's the one—most likely the only one—without doors, windows, a stairway or other interruptions. In the living room shown, the wall measures 13 ft. 5 in., and the ceiling is a standard 8 ft. With these dimensions, a division of the space into five equal compartments provides the best proportions for the unit.

Since the living room is a modest 13 ft. 5 in. × 18 ft., the wall units should not cut into it too deeply. The design takes only 1 ft. off the length of the room and actually makes it appear larger.

After a 2-ft.-high row of cabinets for the base was decided on, the shelf spacing was laid out with an eye to proportion and the ability to accommodate oversize books and other tall objects for display. The bottom two compartments of each unit are a fixed height. The top three compartments are adjustable in height because the top two shelves are movable.

To make the construction as integral as possible with the room, the 3½-in. crown molding that tops off the bookcase was extended completely around the room.

Constructing the boxes

Once you have divided your wall length by the number of individual units that will go together, you can start constructing the "boxes" of ¾-in. birch plywood. The five boxes in the unit shown are each 32 in. wide and 94½ in. high. The height is 1½ in. short of 8 ft. Since you'll be tipping them to an upright position in the room, do not build them to ceiling height or they won't clear. With this design, the molding covers the 1½-in. gap at the ceiling.

Start by cutting box sides, tops and bottoms and five shelves. The tops, bottoms and fixed shelves are dadoed into the box sides, so they are ¾ in. longer than the adjustable shelves. Cut five backs for the boxes from ¼-in. lauan plywood. The dimensions are 32 in. × 89¼ in. The height has to be only 89¼ in. (94½ minus 5¼ in.) since the backs need not cover all the way to the floor, but only far enough down to provide backs for the base cabinets.

Assemble the boxes using glue and 6d finishing nails driven through the sides and into the fixed shelves, tops and bottoms. For the adjustable shelves, bore two holes ½ in. deep in each side of the boxes to accept standard shelf-support pins at the preferred shelf spacing. You can bore additional holes for different spacing at this time or wait until you may want to move the shelves. Installing the lauan backing on the boxes now will assure that they are assembled square with no racking. Use glue and 4d finishing nails.

All the stiles (H and I) can be attached to the boxes now rather than after they are installed in the room. Glue the 2-in.-wide end stiles (H) to the left and right side boxes as shown in the drawing. Attach with 6d finishing nails. Set the nailheads and fill the holes with wood filler. These extend to within 6 in. of the floor (which is the width of the footboards) and to 2¾ in. of the top of the boxes (the width of the headboards).

Attach the center stiles the same way to all the right sides or all the left sides, depending on the direction you'll be installing the units. This lets each box be slipped behind the stile of its neighbor as you install them.

Making the cabinet doors

The most handsome cabinet door for a wall bookcase of this design is the raised-panel type. Making the 10 raised-panel doors is clearly the most difficult and time-consuming part of the job. Door frame rails and stiles and door panels

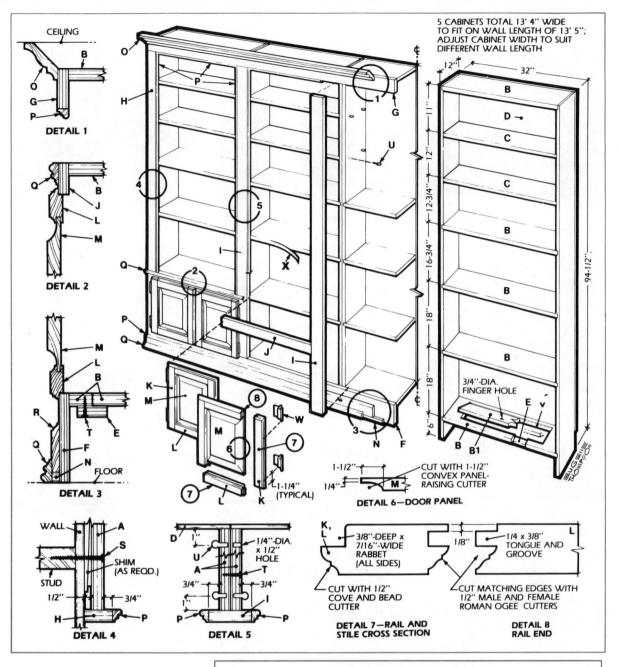

CEILING
DETAIL 1
DETAIL 2
DETAIL 3

5 CABINETS TOTAL 13' 4" WIDE TO FIT ON WALL LENGTH OF 13' 5"; ADJUST CABINET WIDTH TO SUIT DIFFERENT WALL LENGTH

12" 32"
11" 12" 12-3/4" 16-3/4" 18" 18" 6"
94-1/2"

3/4"-DIA. FINGER HOLE

1-1/4" (TYPICAL)

1-1/2"
1/4"
CUT WITH 1-1/2" CONVEX PANEL-RAISING CUTTER
DETAIL 6—DOOR PANEL

WALL
A
S
SHIM (AS REQD.)
STUD
1/2" 3/4"
DETAIL 4

D 1"
1/4"-DIA. x 1/2" HOLE
3/4" 3/4"
1"
DETAIL 5

K,
L,
3/8"-DEEP x 7/16"-WIDE RABBET (ALL SIDES)
CUT WITH 1/2" COVE AND BEAD CUTTER
DETAIL 7—RAIL AND STILE CROSS SECTION

1/8"
1/4 x 3/8" TONGUE AND GROOVE
CUT MATCHING EDGES WITH 1/2" MALE AND FEMALE ROMAN OGEE CUTTERS
DETAIL 8 RAIL END

MATERIALS LIST BOOKCASE WALL

Key	No.	Size and description (use)
A	10	¾ x 11¾ x 94½" plywood (side)
B	25	¾ x 11¾ x 31¾" plywood (top, bottom, fixed shelf)
B1	1	¾ x 9½ x 21½" cutout (hatch)
C	10	¾ x 11¾ x 30½" plywood (adjustable shelf)
D	5	¼ x 32 x 89¼" plywood (back)
E	1	¾ x 2 x 30½" plywood (hatch stop)
F	2	¾ x 6 x 80½" plywood (baseboard)
G	2	¾ x 2¾ x 80½" plywood (headboard)
H	2	¾ x 2 x 85¾" plywood (end style)
I	4	¾ x 3 x 85¾" plywood (center style)
J	5	¾ x 2 x 29" plywood (rail)
K	20	¹³⁄₁₆ x 2¼ x 16¾" poplar (door style)
L	20	¹³⁄₁₆ x 2¼ x 11⅛" poplar (door rail)
M	10	¹³⁄₁₆ x 11¼ x 13" poplar (door panel)
N	2	½ x ¾ x 80½" plywood (filler strip)
O	14 ft.	¹¹⁄₁₆ x 3⅝" crown molding
P	80 ft.	⅝ x ¾" base cap molding
Q	28 ft.	⅝ x 1⅜" base cap molding
R	14 ft.	½ x 3¼" colonial base molding
S	As reqd.	3" No. 10 fh screws
T	As reqd.	1¼" No. 10 fh screws
U	40	Shelf support pins
V	1	1½ x 21" continuous hinge
W	20	
X	As reqd.	Birch plywood veneer tape

Misc.: Carpenter's glue; shim shingles; 4d and 6d finishing nails; 1" finishing brads; 220-grit sandpaper; wood filler; enamel primer; semigloss enamel paint.

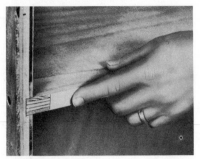

VENEER TAPE covers exposed edges of the birch plywood that is used to build boxes.

FIRST BOX of five is placed in position in left-hand corner of room: others follow in line.

AFTER CUTTING and attaching 3-in.-wide stiles to bridge box edges, cut the rails to fit.

SPACE BETWEEN bottom shelf (B on drawing) and floor is usable if a hatch is built in.

TWO EQUAL-LENGTH BASEBOARDS are used at floor. Electrical outlet plate mounts on back.

USE FINISHING NAILS to attach moldings to the interior edges of the stiles and headboards.

CABINET DOOR SCRAP shows assembly of raised panel, rail and stile (see drawing).

ATTACH THE CABINET DOORS with self-closing hinges mounted on the cabinet stile edges.

EXTENDING the wide crown molding around the room completes the built-in look.

are of poplar, which is easy to work and takes a paint finish very well. The door panels are cut on a shaper or radial-arm saw with a convex panel-raising cutter. The rail and stile glue joints are cut with a cabinet and cove kit. Or you can use a router with the bits specified in details 7 and 8 in the drawing.

Assemble the doors by gluing together the rails and stiles. Do not glue the door panel in place—it should "float" in the frame grooves to allow for expansion and contraction. Put the completed cabinet doors aside. They'll be hung after the boxes are installed.

Before moving the boxes into the room, you may want to cut "hatches" in the bottoms of one or more of the cabinets for use as hiding places.

Move boxes into position

Move the boxes to your room in the order they'll go up against the wall. Before standing up the left or right box (depending on which way you've decided to do the installation), remove any room moldings that might interfere with a flush fit, and transfer the measurements for locations of wall outlets to the back of the boxes. Cut openings through the backs so the receptacles and wall plates can be remounted on the backs after installation.

As you move each box into position, fasten it to its neighbor using 1¼-in. No. 6 flathead wood screws driven through the box sides. Countersink the screw heads and fill the holes with wood filler. When all the boxes are fastened together, secure the boxes to the walls using 3-in. No. 10 flathead wood screws driven through the case sides and backs and into the wall studs. Two or three screws per unit should be plenty if you hit the studs soundly.

Next, cut and attach the cabinet rails (J) between the stiles. Use glue and 6d finishing nails driven into the shelf behind. Set the nail heads and fill the holes with wood filler. Glue veneer tape to all the plywood edges that will be exposed.

Attach moldings around the stiles using 1-in. finishing brads. Headboards and footboards can be installed at this time. Use 6d finishing nails and glue. Set the nail heads and fill the holes.

Baseboard molding can go on next (unless you are planning to lay carpeting against the unit, in which case you should wait until the carpeting is installed).

Priming and painting

Before installing the cabinet doors and the crown molding, paint the unit, the doors and the molding. Begin by sanding the entire case with 220-grit sandpaper. Remove the dust with a vacuum and tack cloth. Before applying two coats of enamel, prime the unit, doors, and molding with enamel undercoat mixed with tint.

Finishing the project

Install the cabinet doors using a ¹⁄₁₆-in.-thick piece of wood or a scrap piece of plastic laminate between the left and right doors of each box. This leaves just enough room for smooth opening and closing. If your doors are a little too tight for the opening, sand the edges where they meet for the proper clearance. If they are a little loose, use shim scrap behind the hinges on the left and right sides to get the dimensions.

You may find that packing books wall to wall in your new addition will give the room too much of a library or lawyer's office look. Relief can be provided with small lamps in one or more compartments and the use of framed prints and other favorite objects.

Inside-the-wall bookcase

■ WHEN FLUSH in the wall, bookshelves not only take on a built-in look but have a way of transforming an uninviting wall into a dramatic center of interest. More important, perhaps, they don't interfere with room furnishings.

Almost any wall will lend itself to built-in bookshelves, but an inside wall presents fewer problems.

The bookshelf wall you see here was built along an inside wall of a family room, which separates the room from a foyer. Since it was a divider wall, a planter was added at the end, filled with greens and spotlighted from above. Use this idea if the design of your wall lends itself to it.

Where the wall is plastered, it isn't necessary to remove the lath and plaster. The wall shown was paneled to begin with, and it was no problem to pull off the plywood paneling. Exposed studs do make it easier to get at any wiring to bring it out to the new wall.

You can make the niche any size you want, of course. Start by nailing a 44¼×67¼-in. sheet of hardboard horizontally (and level) to the studs 34 in. up from the plate. Then block the ends with 2 × 4s. Next, frame the panel all around the edge with 1 × 2s and nail them at points where they cross the studs.

When this is done, you can start to frame the second wall. First nail a 2 × 4 soleplate to the floor, locating it 9¾ in. out from the first wall. Then nail another 2 × 4 plate to the ceiling. You will need to prop it against the ceiling with a couple of studs and plumb it so it aligns with the bottom plate. If you're lucky to have the ceiling joists run at right angles to the wall, you can spike the top plate to them. If they run parallel and miss the top plate, you'll have to anchor it with toggle bolts.

The front opening of the niche is framed to coincide with the 1 × 2s at the back; whatever they measure from inside to inside, the opening at the front is made to measure the same. Your particular framing may vary somewhat from that shown in the drawings, but essentially it's framed as detailed. A 2 × 4 header is placed across the top of the opening, a 2 × 4 plate across the bottom and short studs installed above and below.

Short blocks are cut to fit between the back and front wall for support. These are 2 × 4s at the corners and 1 × 2s elsewhere. You can dado

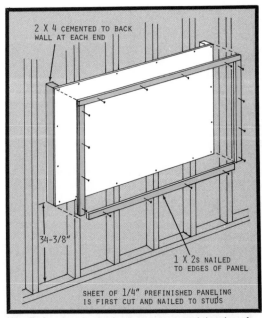

2 X 4 CEMENTED TO BACK WALL AT EACH END

34-3/8"

1 X 2s NAILED TO EDGES OF PANEL

SHEET OF 1/4" PREFINISHED PANELING IS FIRST CUT AND NAILED TO STUDS

If wall size permits, make the recess equal the size of a 4x8-ft. panel and you won't have to cut it. Where the bookcase wall is to match a painted room, plasterboard would be used to line the recess and face the wall. Here, regular plaster bead would be used to frame the outer corners of the recess.

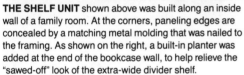**THE SHELF UNIT** shown above was built along an inside wall of a family room. At the corners, paneling edges are concealed by a matching metal molding that was nailed to the framing. As shown on the right, a built-in planter was added at the end of the bookcase wall, to help relieve the "sawed-off" look of the extra-wide divider shelf.

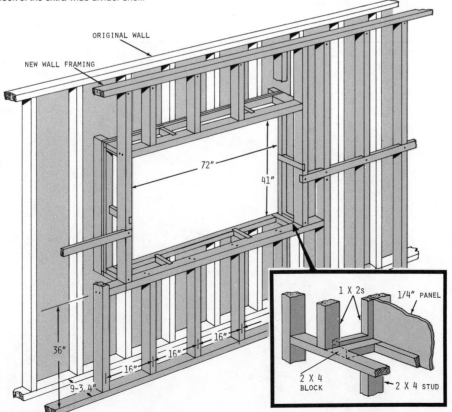

ORIGINAL WALL

NEW WALL FRAMING

72"

41"

36"

9-3, 4"

16"

16"

16"

1 X 2s

1/4" PANEL

2 X 4 BLOCK

2 X 4 STUD

these into the front wall or you can simply butt them—it's not that critical. If you want to notch them, do it when cutting the framing members. Finally, 1×2 blocks are added to the four 2×4 blocks to create gluing surfaces.

There are any number of prefinished plywood panels from which to pick. If you're going to paint the wall, you'll want to line and face it with plasterboard, then tape and fill the joints.

The narrow pieces that line the niche are ripped 9⅝ in. wide to allow ⅛ in. for expansion. Cut and install the end pieces first, sawing them a little short. Use a panel adhesive to cement them in place.

Cut and cement the top and bottom pieces in place. Like the ends, they're butted against the back wall and cut to fit snug against the end panels. Sticks wedged between them, at the front and back, hold them in place while the cement sets. Any adhesive smears can be easily removed with a cloth dipped in rubber-cement thinner.

You're now ready to panel the wall. First you must cover the exposed edges of the lining with an aluminum outside-corner molding mitered at the corners like a picture frame. This material saws easily, comes in 8-ft. lengths and matches the color of the paneling. A flange permits the molding to be nailed in place so the nails are later

concealed by the paneling. Applying the paneling involves cutting the plans to fit and cementing them to the studs. Special metal clips are provided to self-space the joints, since they should not be forced tightly together. You can also use the thickness of a dime to keep them properly spaced.

The shelf brackets shown are the kind that need no vertical standards. They're designed to hook in slots in paneling. Simply cut slots in the hardboard, using a tiny burr in a hand grinder and a template to space the slots evenly. You can arrange the shelves as you wish. Two 10×48-in. ready-made shelves, staggered as shown, provided ample room for books and bric-a-brac in the arrangement shown.

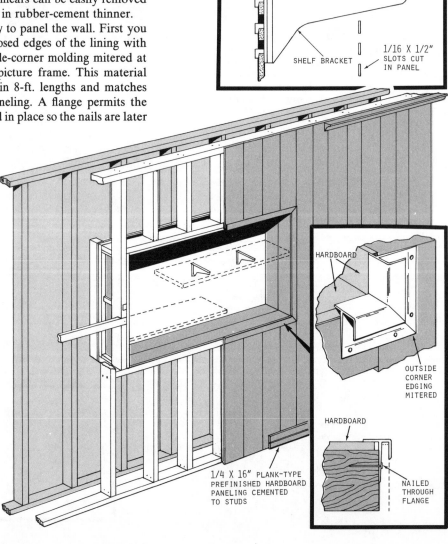

IN THIS system, aluminum standards and brackets are combined with prefinished boards.

YOU CAN use pegboard almost anywhere. Special brackets support shelves of various sizes.

All kinds of book shelves

College student's standby

Perhaps the simplest and least expensive system of book shelves is the college student's old standby: stacks of concrete blocks with shelf boards between. It's a strong, durable and cheap system, but the blocks themselves take up a considerable amount of room, and the shelving setup is not exactly a decorator's dream.

Another possibility is utility shelving made of perforated steel. A good utility shelving system is about the strongest system made, but most of us don't need *that* much strength in our living room or study. And again it's not very attractive.

Decorative utility shelving

However, several manufacturers of utility shelving are extending the limits of their products into the area of interior decor. They've done this by adding bright colors to lightweight utility shelving. The color selection is wide, including red, blue, yellow, brown, green, white and almond. Low in cost, these smart-looking shelves make attractive book shelves and utility storage space in student study rooms, home offices, laundry rooms and other areas where strong but attractive shelving is required.

When most of us think of book shelves, though, we think of what has become the standard system in most homes: slotted steel wall supports, with thin steel brackets that hold wood, plywood or particle-board shelves.

Many choices

You have a wide choice of systems, and usually a choice of colors and finishes within each system.

Prefinished shelf boards are marketed in standard lengths and widths from 8×24 to 12×72 in., though not all sizes are available from every manufacturer. You can buy boards prefinished in walnut, butcher block, pecan, black, white and several solid colors. Most surfaces are melamine, which is handsome and stands up well under regular cleaning. But note that it does not have the durability or scratch resistance of plastic laminate.

HOW ARE THESE massive oak-plank shelves anchored? Lag bolts enter the oak from the other side of the wall, passing totally through the studs. Lagbolt heads were countersunk and plastered over.

Shelfboards for your own system

One manufacturer marks its markets "Appearance Boards" in lengths to 12 ft. They are available in plain or wood-grain finishes. They not only are applicable to standard shelving systems, but are well suited to the construction of a shelf system of your own design.

hardware consisting of steel (or aluminum) slotted standards. Brackets are keyed to fit the slots. In such a system, if the wall is vertical the shelves inevitably are horizontal, back to front. If you are careful to mount the supports at exactly the same height, the shelves are flat and level.

Make a mental note that in most of these systems there is a top and bottom to the supports. Many a homemaker has carefully screwed his supports into the studs, only to find that one or more of them are upside down. The slots look the same no matter which end is at the top, so be careful.

You don't have to buy prefinished boards in order to use these handsome standards and brackets. You can cut your own shelves of plywood and cover the edges with pine strips. Or if you want especially attractive and durable shelves you can apply a plastic laminate to particle-board shelves. The result will be the most attractive shelves you can build, and you have your choice of a tremendous number of patterns.

In fastening the standards to the wall, keep three things in mind:

First, the standards should be located so shelves will not protrude very far beyond the brackets. Three inches is a good measure of thumb. This assures that a heavy object on the end of a shelf will not tip up the opposite end. Naturally the location of the appropriate wall stud may affect how far the shelf extends beyond the end bracket.

Second, be sure that the screws provided with the standards do indeed penetrate into studs. Magnetic and electronic stud locators are available. Usually the simplest way to locate studs is to examine the baseboard. The nails that hold it in most cases are driven into studs.

Occasionally it is impossible to locate a support over a stud. In such a case use a suitable wall anchor.

Third, make certain the shelves are level. The first step is to attach one standard to the wall with the brackets at exactly the right heights. Then rest one end of a level atop the standard (or against the bottom), center the bubble in the glass, and then hold the level tight to the wall. Now press the second standard against the wall at the desired distance, and mark the position of the top screw hole. Bore a hole for the top screw and drive it in place, drawing the standard tight to the wall before marking other hole locations.

Now install the brackets. Don't forget to take the thickness of the shelves into consideration as you determine the spacing of the brackets. Once you have located the brackets in one standard, you can "count slots" to make sure all the other brackets are properly positioned.

Tap brackets into place

As you install each bracket, tap it on the top, close to the standard, with a hammer to make certain that it is well seated in the slots. The design of the bracket does not allow you to see whether it is seated properly. A tap with the hammer assures that the bracket is securely locked in its designed position and will not slip out from normal home vibrations.

There's one trick you can use if you want particularly attractive shelves. This eliminates the gap all along the back of each shelf (the protruding standard prevents you from installing the shelf flush with the wall). If you want to solve this problem, and at the same time eliminate the protruding ends of the shelf brackets, buy brackets the next size smaller than your shelf boards.

After installing the hardware, place each shelf in position. Mark the rear edge of each shelf for notching for the standards; mark the bottom side for the projecting front tip of each bracket. Cut the notches and drill ⅜-in. holes for the bracket tips. Reinstall the shelves flush with the wall.

This kind of installation requires considerably more work, but it is neater, slightly stronger, and somewhat cheaper. The smaller size brackets are less expensive, and if you need a good many of them for your particular installation, you'll save a significant amount of money.

The standard system of wall shelving offers great versatility. You set up your own system of shelves just the way you want it. You are not locked into a specific shelf spacing or arrangement; indeed you can also have shelves of various widths by buying brackets of various sizes. Frequently homeowners will install a wider shelf at the bottom or the top to hold those highway atlases and photo albums that seem to fit nowhere else.

You can also change the arrangement anytime you wish simply by moving brackets to new positions. And for a thorough cleaning, you can lift the shelves right off the wall.

If you prefer the look and warmth of real, all-wood shelving, you have a couple of options. You can buy handsome, ready-made, prefinished shelving in one of several styles, or you can build your own shelves, perhaps copying an authentic period piece. One manufacturer produces solid wood shelves and brackets in five distinctive styles to harmonize with Tudor, Colonial, Early American, provincial, traditional and contemporary interiors. Each bracket has a hardware strip attached, which keys over the heads of screws driven into wall studs. Installation is simple and easy. The same brackets can be attached to matching wood standards to visually unify several shelves. Bracket-supported mantel boards are also available with this system.

Wall anchors

Whenever you hang book shelves on a wall you must be certain your screws have a solid hold. Books on even a short shelf have tremendous weight. Wall anchors help assure a solid grip on the wall.

The best anchor of all, of course, is a 2x4 stud inside the wall. If you can screw into a stud, whatever you hang will almost certainly stay in place. But in hanging book shelves it's not always possible to find studs exactly where you need them because the spacing is wrong. And of course a solid masonry wall presents still another and more difficult problem.

The simplest and most economical wall anchor is a plastic sleeve that has a slight taper to it. Sleeves vary in length from ¾-in. upward. You drill a slightly undersize hole in the plasterboard, tap a sleeve into it, then drive your screw into the sleeve. As the screw penetrates the sleeve it expands it, forcing it tight into the plasterboard.

With plastic sleeves you can use the matching wood screws furnished with your shelving standards, but any sheet-metal screw will work with this type of anchor. A similar anchor made of lead is designed for solid masonry walls.

Of course you must drill holes to use these plastic or lead anchors; the packaging usually tells you what size drill bit to use.

If you ever decide to relocate your shelves, you can lift out the anchors with a screwdriver blade. Plug the holes with patching plaster, sand lightly, and the wall will show no sign that it once supported a system of book shelves.

Plastic wall anchors should be used to hold only relatively light weights. If you plan an extensive system of book shelves, or want to display particularly heavy objects, use toggle bolts or expansion anchors usually called Molly bolts.

A toggle bolt is easily identified by the pair of spring-loaded wings threaded onto it. It is a heavy-duty anchor for hollow walls. Sizes range from 2 to 6 inches.

Bookends personalized by you

■ PHOTOGRAPHIC bookends will add a novel touch to your bookshelves, particularly when they are cutouts of members of the family or friends. And they're ideal for Christmas gift-giving.

Though children make great subjects, grown-ups can get into the act, too. It is easy to photo-graph your subject posed in a holding or pushing position, and any background will do because it will be cut out. Pose the person against a wall or other vertical prop to represent the books. This helps to obtain a convincing, natural stance. Enlargements can be single or double weight, glossy or matte; it's not too important. Mounting can be on hardboard or ordinary fir plywood.

For permanence, use contact cement to mount the prints, but avoid lumps or bubbles in cement because they show through on the print surface. A better way to mount the pictures is with dry-mounting tissue.

Standard photo dry-mounting tissue doesn't work too well for mounting pictures on materials

1. MATERIALS AND TOOLS used: pictures, plywood, electric iron, scissors, kraft paper, mounting tissue.

2. SPOT-TACK TISSUE to back of the photo using point of the iron. This will keep pieces from shifting.

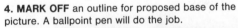
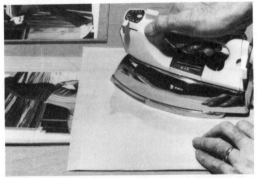

3. USE LOW-HEAT IRON and wrapping-paper buffer. Hold the paper and slowly pass iron over the "sandwich."

5. SET JIGSAW tilting table at a slight angle so the cutout edge bevels slightly to back (i.e., undercut).

4. MARK OFF an outline for proposed base of the picture. A ballpoint pen will do the job.

6. EXPOSED PORTION of the groove for photo cutout is easily concealed by a glued-in wood spline.

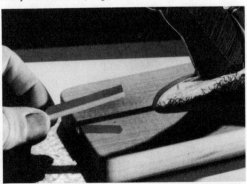

OTHER SUBJECTS AND POSES

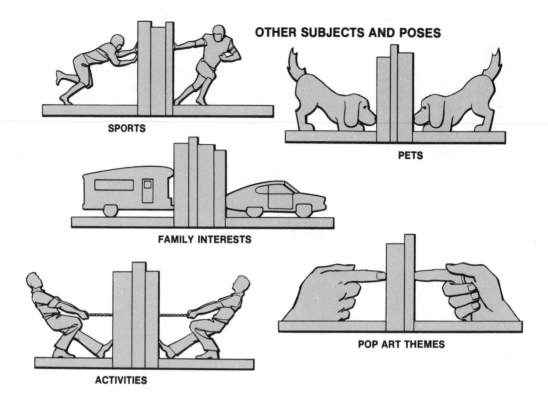

SPORTS

PETS

FAMILY INTERESTS

ACTIVITIES

POP ART THEMES

other than cardboard, but there is a special tissue that does. It's sold at photo and art supply houses. This low-temperature tissue adheres well to wood and requires no special equipment—only an ordinary electric iron.

Set the iron for 180° and pass it over the board and back of the print to preheat. Attach a tissue to the back of the print by spot-tacking it once or twice with the tip of the iron. Tacked spots should be no bigger than ½ in. If the tissue extends beyond the edge of the print, trim it flush. Place the tacked print on the board and cover it with a sheet of clean wrapping paper.

Now apply heat by making a few slow passes with the iron. A total heat time of 5 to 10 seconds for a given area should do. Since the tissue sets while cooling, place the mounting under a flat weight after heating.

If you don't own a power jigsaw, you can make the cutouts by hand with a coping saw. Either way, use a very fine-tooth blade. Before cutting, decide on a suitable design for ending the picture at the bottom and mark this outline on the picture with a ballpoint pen. Also, leave about ¼ in. below the usable part of the picture to serve as a mounting tab which sets into the wood base. (See details below.)

Size and shape of the base is optional but it must have a "tongue" long enough to reach under three or four books to hold properly. Thin galvanized (22-ga.) sheet metal with edges smoothed and felt cloth glued on the bottom serves nicely.

BASE DETAILS

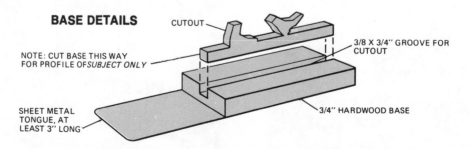

CUTOUT

3/8 X 3/4" GROOVE FOR CUTOUT

NOTE: CUT BASE THIS WAY FOR PROFILE OF *SUBJECT ONLY*

SHEET METAL TONGUE, AT LEAST 3" LONG

3/4" HARDWOOD BASE

Initial bookends

■ HERE'S A GIFT that is as personal as it can be—bookends of a friend's first and last initials. Letters C, O, U, J and V must be altered a bit to provide flat bottoms for attaching sheet-metal bases to the bookends. The project provides a good way to use up scrap wood and pieces of plastic laminate.

Oak plastic laminate was used on the face of the letters shown here and the rest was painted. Cement the laminate to the wood and tape a paper pattern of the initial (enlarged from the drawing below) to the laminate before bandsawing.

SANDING the bandsawed edges of the letters goes a lot faster with a band sander, of course, but it can be done by hand with the sandpaper wrapped around a dowel or block.

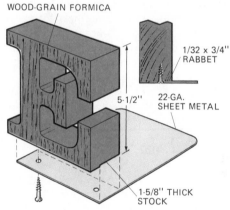

WOOD-GRAIN FORMICA

1/32 x 3/4" RABBET

5-1/2"

22-GA. SHEET METAL

1-5/8" THICK STOCK

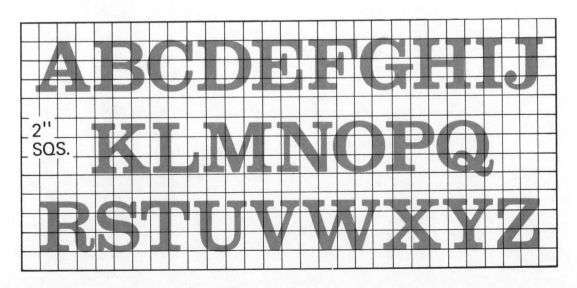

2" SQS.

ABCDEFGHIJ
KLMNOPQ
RSTUVWXYZ

Book-go-round for your desk

■ HERE'S A DESK carousel for books that rotates with a flick of the finger for convenient access to any one of four compartments.

For good looks, cabinet-grade mahogany plywood is used. The unit is dimensioned so that all pieces can be cut from a standard ½-in. x 2-ft.-sq. sheet of plywood. (Use a scrap piece of plywood without a veneer for the 8-in.-sq. base piece because it does not show; the leftover piece of mahogany-veneer plywood can then be saved for another project.)

First cut the two crosspieces with slots in each piece exactly as wide as the stock is thick so they will fit tightly without using glue. (Because ½-in. stock is specified, slots should be ½-in. wide, but sometimes the standard thickness dimension is not exact.) Cut four endpieces, mark and saw a curve on one corner of each as shown in the drawing on the opposite page and sand.

Glue and nail one pair of endpieces to each crosspiece using two 1¼-in. finishing nails per joint. Set nailheads, fill with wood filler to match mahogany veneer and sand. Join notched crosspieces, turn upside down and glue and nail bottom piece in place. Drill 1-in.-dia. hole in base piece, positioned as shown in drawing at right. Screw bearing to base piece and then to bottom piece by rotating base piece with 1-in.-dia. hole to gain access to screw holes in upper plate of bearing as shown in photos at right.

Apply a clear finish on all surfaces. Edges should also be finished with paint or flexible wood tape that's stained to match the mahogany veneer.

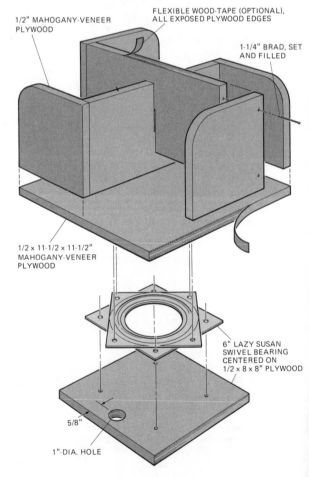

1/2" MAHOGANY-VENEER PLYWOOD

FLEXIBLE WOOD-TAPE (OPTIONAL), ALL EXPOSED PLYWOOD EDGES

1-1/4" BRAD, SET AND FILLED

1/2 x 11-1/2 x 11-1/2" MAHOGANY-VENEER PLYWOOD

6" LAZY SUSAN SWIVEL BEARING CENTERED ON 1/2 x 8 x 8" PLYWOOD

5/8"

1"-DIA. HOLE

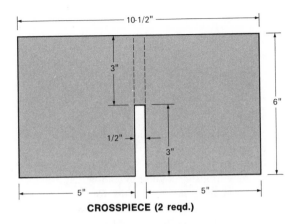

CROSSPIECE (2 reqd.)

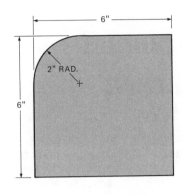

ENDPIECE (4 reqd.)

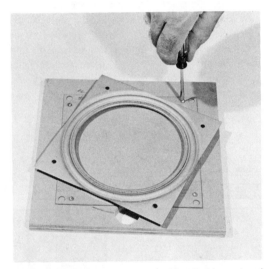

BOTTOM PLATE of 6-in.-sq. swivel bearing is centered and screwed to plywood base piece.

PIECES ARE TEST FIT, endpieces nailed to crosspieces, latter fitted together and the bottom attached.

UPPER PLATE of bearing is attached to bottom piece of inverted bookrack through access hole in base.

MAHOGANY-VENEER plywood is treated with a clear finish, edges with paint or flexible wood tape.

Colonial bookrack

■ A HANDSOME BUT SELDOM SEEN PIECE these days is the small bookrack that was set upon a chest or other piece of furniture. My version is a replica of those that were found in almost every American home a century or so ago.

Except for the spindles and dowels, the entire piece can be made of pine. However, if you prefer, the rack can be cut from hardwood, such as walnut or cherry which have particularly attractive grain patterns.

Start by making a full-size pattern of the base and, after cutting and shaping, lay out the dowel and spindle locations. The dowels can be turned on your lathe, but if you prefer, the commercial hardwood dowels that are available at lumberyards will do the trick; if you use the latter you'll just have to spend a little more time staining to insure a good overall match.

Assembling the rack calls for a little planning. The nature of the project requires that a number of pieces be assembled simultaneously. First, assemble the top rails as one unit. Then saw kerfs in the lower ends of the dowels and assemble the dowels and corner spindles to the base and top rail. A small screw driven up into each kerfed dowel wedges them securely. A little glue will provide additional support and guarantee a sturdy bookrack.

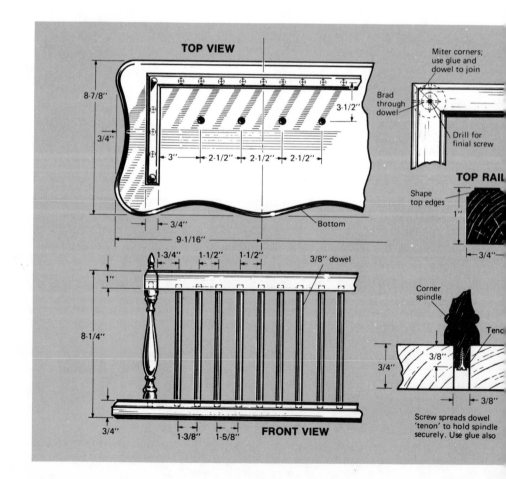

BOOK SUPPORT

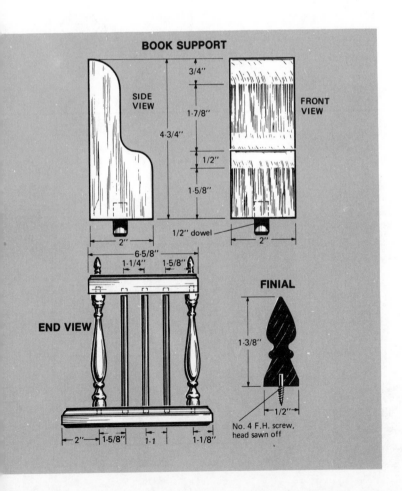

SIDE VIEW

FRONT VIEW

3/4"

1-7/8"

4-3/4"

1/2"

1-5/8"

2"

2"

1/2" dowel

END VIEW

6-5/8"

1-1/4"

1-5/8"

2"   1-5/8"   1-1   1-1/8"

FINIAL

1-3/8"

1/2"

No. 4 F.H. screw,
head sawn off

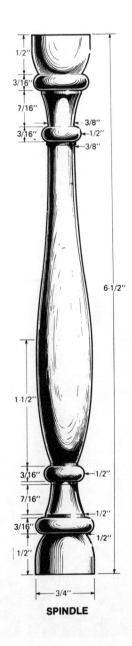

1/2"

3/16"

7/16"

3/8"

3/16"

1/2"

3/8"

6-1/2"

1-1/2"

3/16"

1/2"

7/16"

1/2"

3/16"

1/2"

1/2"

3/4"

SPINDLE

Colonial bookstand

■ THIS EARLY American bookstand will cost very little to make. If you own a lathe, you'll enjoy turning the centerpost; if not, you can buy it already turned.

To make it, cut the shaped shelf pieces and legs with a bandsaw, sabre saw or jigsaw, then round off the edges either by hand or with a router.

When drilling the dowel holes in the legs, be sure they are bored straight and true. Then shape the butting edges so they fit the post. This can be done by wrapping sandpaper around the post and using it as a form. Use dowel-locating centers to transfer the leg holes to the post. The center post is attached to the shelf by a 4-in. disc. Screws are used in counterbored holes to attach the sides of the shelf and the holes are capped with decorative wood buttons.

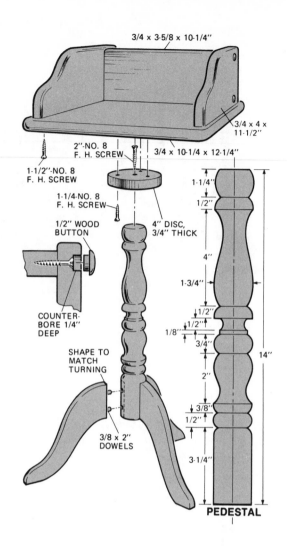

3/4 x 3-5/8 x 10-1/4"
3/4 x 4 x 11-1/2"
3/4 x 10-1/4 x 12-1/4"
2"-NO. 8 F. H. SCREW
1-1/2"-NO. 8 F. H. SCREW
1-1/4-NO. 8 F. H. SCREW
1/2" WOOD BUTTON
4" DISC, 3/4" THICK
COUNTER-BORE 1/4" DEEP
SHAPE TO MATCH TURNING
3/8 x 2" DOWELS

1-1/4"
1/2"
4"
1-3/4"
1/2"
1/2"
1/8"
3/4"
2"
3/8"
1/2"
3-1/4"
14"

PEDESTAL

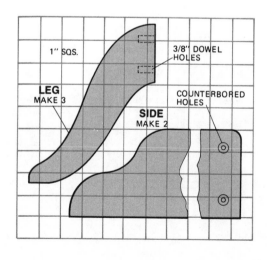

1" SQS.
3/8" DOWEL HOLES
LEG MAKE 3
SIDE MAKE 2
COUNTERBORED HOLES

Cookbook caddy

■ THIS HANDSOME SHELF will add a touch of interest to your kitchen and keep your cookbooks handy at the same time. Its drawer can store recipes galore.

There are no fancy joints to bother with; nothing but butt joints, glued and nailed, are used. The back and the drawer interior are cut from plywood, but ½-in. solid pine is used for the rest. Set your rip fence to make 12-in. cuts and run all at one time to insure a perfect fit for all inside pieces and to save yourself time. Saw the curves, then use your router with a ¼-round bit to round the edges where indicated. Sand all surfaces as smooth as you will want them before you begin the assembly.

Assemble the parts with glue and 1½-in. finishing nails in this order: First attach the base apron to the drawer shelf. Then attach the back to both shelves and add the sides. Set the nailheads and fill the holes. Make the plywood drawer as a box with four sides and a bottom, then add the pine false front and the knob. For an interesting finish, that is not too difficult, try a wood graining or antiquing kit.

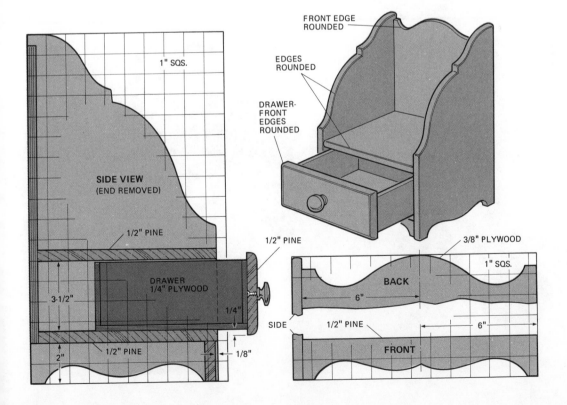

From bottles to fancy glassware

■ THERE IS SOMETHING UNIVERSAL in the appeal of an attractive, fancy bottle—its color, size and shape—and for years people have tried to make things from bottles. The big bugaboo was cutting them. Many makeshift and primitive methods were used, including the old trick of soaking a string in kerosene, tying it around the bottle, igniting the string and then plunging the bottle in water to fracture it at the string. There was no guarantee the method would work, and seldom did you wind up with a clean, even break.

New cutting equipment

The current bottle-cutting craze has changed all that. Now simple cutting equipment available in kits has taken all the guesswork out of cutting a bottle. It's so simple you can make a clean, even cut every time. Wine and beer bottles, even large glass jugs, which were normally thrown away, are being converted into all kinds of attractive and useful pieces of glassware such as you see displayed here. Tall wine bottles make graceful bud vases when the tops are cut off and cemented to shallow sections of the bottoms. A gallon jug cut near the top and then cemented to a base cut from a quart bottle becomes a pretty fruit bowl. The bottom part of the jug will serve as a candy dish when cut 2 in. deep. The lower half of a straight-sided liquor bottle makes a perfect hurricane lamp when fitted with a stubby candle. Ashtrays for the patio or porch can be made from the bottoms of bottles. The possibilities are practically endless.

Beer bottles make good practice bottles as they cut and polish easily. Wine bottles offer an interesting range of shapes, colors and sizes. The glass is of better quality than beer bottles and thicker. Burgundy, Bordeaux or champagne bottles, which have dimpled bottoms, make extra-attractive pieces.

THE STYLECRAFT KIT includes a bottle cutter, candle, strips of coarse-grade and fine-grade silicone-carbide paper and a vial of carbide grits. The candle is used to heat the etch. The glass is then cracked with an ice cube. The paper and grit are used to grind and polish the cut edge.

Basically, there are two types of bottle-cutting kits on the market: One cuts the bottle vertically, the other, horizontally. The vertical cutter uses the top of the bottle as a guide to swing the glass cutter around the outside of the bottle. The horizontal cutter uses the bottom of the bottle as a guide, the glass cutter remains stationary and the scoring is done by rotating the bottle around the cutter.

Of the two methods, the horizontal one is easier. You don't have to go through a lot of adjusting and fussing to cut bottles of different diameters; you just cradle the bottle against a stop and turn it. Once the stop is set for height, you can't miss when making matched sets of glasses—all will be of uniform size. There is also less waste. If two sections don't break cleanly when you're using a horizontal cutter, you can continue to salvage the base of the bottle since you don't need the neck to recut it.

● **Cutting.** The key to successful bottle cutting is the scoring. Only a *light etch should be made, and only one time around the bottle*. It is important that the adjustable cutting wheel always be at a right angle to the glass surface to assure a straight cut and a flat edge. It's also important to put a drop of oil on the cutter each time you cut a bottle.

To score a bottle, remove the label and place the bottle in the cradle on the rollers with the bottom against the backstop. Grip the bottle with both hands as shown and with a constant, even pressure, turn the bottle toward you without stopping. A jerky motion will cause the cutter to skip and make an uneven etch. A slight crunching sound will signal one time around the bottle and when you hear it, stop. Avoid retracing the original score as this will chip the glass and damage the cutter. To assure perfect alignment of the

1. THE BOTTLE is cut by placing it on the cutter rollers and rotating it one turn to etch the glass lightly.

2. THE ETCHED LINE is heated by holding the bottle over the candle flame and rotating it two or three times.

3. THE GLASS is cracked neatly along the etched line by chilling the heated glass with an ice cube.

4. THE EDGE is polished by dipping it in water and rubbing on a flat surface sprinkled with carbide grit.

etch from beginning to end, it is important to keep the bottom of the bottle in contact with the backstop as you turn it.

• **Heating.** To separate the bottle at the etched line you first heat the line with a candle. Hold the bottle horizontally over the candle about ¼ in. away from the tip of the flame, and slowly rotate it three or four times in one direction. Then turn it three or four more times at a faster pace. The glass should feel hot to the touch, but not too hot to handle.

• **Cooling.** Now place the bottle in an upright position and, before the bottle cools, rub an ice cube around the etched line several times until the etch becomes a crack. If the etched line has been properly heated, a crack will start to form the instant the ice touches the glass and will

continue around the bottle as it is chilled by the ice, resulting in a comparatively smooth fracture. The smoothness of the edge is very important because the grinding of the edge is the hardest part of bottle-cutting.

If the two sections fail to part with a slight tug, don't force them; reheat the etch and try again. Sometimes it's necessary to repeat the heating and cooling steps several times depending on the thickness of the glass.

• **Polishing.** The final step is polishing the cut edge. This is done by first rubbing the inside and outside edges lightly with the coarse carborundum paper. Then carbide grit is sprinkled on a flat, hard surface such as a piece of window glass. The cut bottle is dipped in water and placed on the polishing surface. Start to grind in a circular motion. After a short time (10 to 15 minutes, depending on the thickness of the glass) the edge will become perfectly flat and take on a "frosted" appearance. While you're grinding, keep the rim of the glass wet at all times—the water will make the grinding action more effective. Sprinkle the carbide grit in a circle rather than concentrate it in one spot. Now you are ready to round the sharp edges with the fine-grit paper, dipping it in water as you rub.

• **Cementing.** Epoxy adhesive is used to cement the top of one bottle to the bottom of another. Mix a small amount of the two-part cement and apply it sparingly. Support the work in an upright position and set aside overnight for the cement to harden. Finally, polish your finished piece with glass wax.

THESE ARE TYPICAL wine, beer and liquor bottles you can turn into handsome and useful pieces of glassware.

Bottling houses

■ MANY OF US HAVE A DREAM HOUSE we planned in detail. One artist has perfected a system for building those dream houses in glass bottles—be they castle or cabin, mansion or Swiss chalet.

Building techniques

The building techniques given here will help you become an architect in miniature:
• Keep your first project simple. It takes practice to work in a confined space with minute material.
• Avoid tinted bottles or those with surfaces that distort your view and cause eyestrain.
• Plan your house before you begin so you won't run out of space at the top. A rough sketch with dimensions will help.
• Prebuilding outside the bottle won't work. Unevenness of the bottle bottom causes a house made outside to be crooked when it is reassembled inside.

Among major tools you'll use are varying lengths of aluminum clothesline wire—some with hat pins to lower wood into place, and others bent into hooks for prying and lifting. Also needed are model-making knives, tweezers, small files, razor saw, clamps, sandpaper and fine paintbrushes.

Use a power saw to cut wood to workable size, and use a small hand saw to cut it exactly. Simulated lathe work is really small doweling rounded with a grinder and carved with a modeler's knife.

Materials required

A bottle is the first necessity. It may be anything from a plain juice jar to a hand-blown decorator-type container.

Several types of wood are used for the house.

Ice cream sticks are perfect for subflooring and roofing. Walnut or fir is good for window frames, doors, joists and paneling. Shingles are veneer. An open-grain wood like oak is used to fashion bricks.

You'll need modeling clay for the base, plus rocks and pebbles for landscaping or embedding in a modeling-clay fireplace. Other materials are plastic, glass, screening, cardboard and Styrofoam.

Epoxy glue cements the house foundation to

the bottle. White glue is strong enough for construction. Other materials include wood stain and quick-drying tempera paint.

Building the house

First, secure four ½-in. corner cubes inside the bottle to the bottom with epoxy. Then place crosspieces—ice cream sticks work well—to form a square. When glue holding the blocks has dried, press modeling clay around the foundation to the desired level. Lower landscaping rocks and pebbles into the bottle on masking tape; press them in the clay.

A subflooring of ice cream sticks or other thin strips comes next, followed by the first-floor uprights. Cut one to approximate length, lower it into place with a needled wire, measure, pull it out and cut it to the exact length. Measure again

and modify if needed. Then use this as a master for other pieces. Glue each piece, lower it and twist the board free from the wire.

Once all first-floor uprights are placed, add horizontal pieces for windows and door frames. Plastic or acrylic windows and prepainted siding finish the first floor.

Unlike building a real house, finish one floor before you move on to the next. Each additional floor is built just like the first one.

When you reach the top, glue rafters in place and cover them with a subroofing of flat sticks. Then cut tiny rectangular veneer shingles, whittle them at one end to form a wedge shape so they rest in place and glue them to the roof.

Decorative touches will depend on the style of the house. Once you've mastered the structural basics, there's no limit to what you can build.

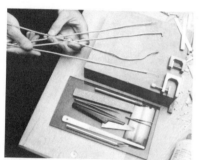

TOOLS THE ARTIST uses: aluminum wire, model knives, file, tweezers, clamps, saw and sandpaper. Below, lowering wood into place.

SUBFLOORING and first floor uprights are in place and fireplace is complete (above). Same construction steps are used (below) on second floor.

RUSTIC HOUSES and cabins are popular subjects. These wood veneer shingles are individually carved.

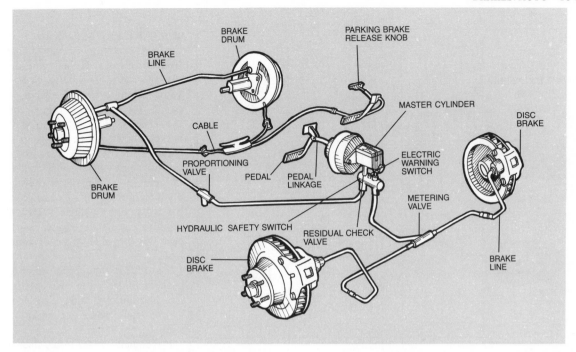

Brake system troubleshooting guide

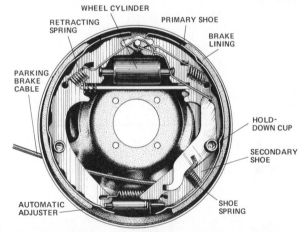

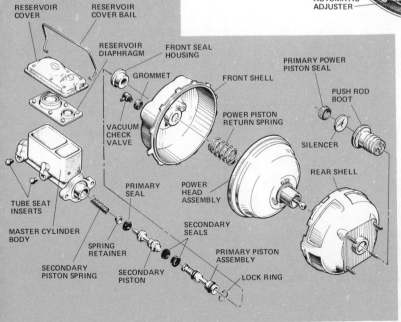

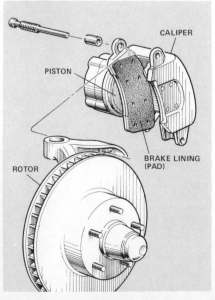

TROUBLESHOOTING BRAKES

CAUSE \ PROBLEM	Excessive pedal travel.	Pedal travel gradually increases.	Excessive pedal effort.	Brakes slow to respond.	Brakes slow to release.	Brakes drag.	Uneven (side to side pull) brake action.	Uneven (front to rear grab) brake action.	Scraping noise.	Brakes squeak when applied.	Brakes squeak during stop.	Brake chatter (roughness).	Brakes groan at end of stop.	Brake warning light glows during stop.
Leaking brake line or brake line connection.	*	**						*						**
Leaking wheel cylinder or master cylinder piston seal.	*	**					*							*
Leaking master cylinder.	*	**												*
Air trapped in brake system.	**							*						**
Contaminated or improper brake fluid.				*	*	*								
Leaking brake booster vacuum system.			**											
Restricted air passage in brake booster power head.			*	**	*									
Damaged brake booster power head.			*	*	*	*								
Improperly assembled brake booster power head valving.			*	*	*	**								
Worn brake lining.			*				*	*	*	*	*		*	
Uneven brake lining wear.	*						*	*	*	*	**		*	*
Glazed brake lining.			**	*			*	*	*	*	*			
Incorrect lining.							*	*	*	*	*		*	
Contaminated brake lining.							**	**	*	*	*		*	
Too much brake lining dust.			*				**	**		*	**		*	
Scored drum(s) or rotor(s).							*	*		*	*	**		*
Drums out of round.											*	**		
Rotors out of parallel.												**		
Excessive rotor run-out.												*		
Damaged automatic adjusters.	*					*	*	*						*
Incorrect wheel cylinder size.			*			*	*							
Weak or incorrect brake shoe springs.				*	**	*		*		**	*	**		
Missing or loose brake-assembly fasteners (cups).	*			*	*	*		*			*	*		‹
Brake-shoe guide insufficiently lubricated.				*	*	*	*	*		**	**			
Restricted brake fluid passage or sticking wheel cylinder piston.		*	*	*	*	*	*	*						
Faulty metering valve.		*		*	*	*	*							*
Brake pedal linkage binding or being interfered with.			*	*	**	**								
Improperly adjusted parking brake.						*								
Tapered or threaded drums.											**			
Incorrect front end alignment.							**							
Incorrect tire pressure.							*	*						
Incorrect wheel bearing adjustment.	*							*				*		
Loose front suspension.							*			**		*	*	
Out-of-balance wheels.												**		
Driver rides brake pedal.	*	*	*			*							*	
Improperly adjusted master cylinder push rod.	*				*	**								*
Sticking wheel cylinder or caliper piston.			*			*	*	*						
Faulty proportioning valve.			*	*	*	*								

■ BRAKE PROBLEMS are one of the most common complaints heard from car owners. To help you identify the cause of malfunctions in your braking system, we have prepared the troubleshooting chart shown at the left. Use it to match brake problems with causes. It includes both disc and drum brakes.

Since some causes are more likely to create a problem than others, a double asterisk (**) indicates probable cause, while a single asterisk (*) signifies a less likely cause. Investigate the probable cause or causes first.

The illustration on the preceding page identifies parts mentioned in the chart and will make it easier for you to troubleshoot the brake system.

It is imperative for safety that the warning signs of a defective braking system are recognized and acted upon at once. A braking system seldom fails suddenly. Rather, it emits a warning for several hundred miles before the situation becomes dangerous.

The most common warning signs are:
- Lighting of the dash brake warning light.
- Harsh noise (a low-pitched squeal on brake application is usually normal).
- Hard pedal.
- Pulsating pedal.
- A pedal that doesn't rise when the self-adjusting mechanism is activated (car moved in Reverse).
- Severe pull when brakes are applied.

Brake system check up

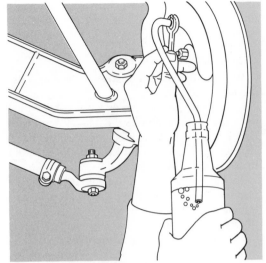

BLEEDING THE BRAKES makes air in the hydraulic system bubble through the container of fluid. Close the bleed valve when the bubbles stop.

■ WE ALL WANT to be sure our car has ample "Go" for our needs. But any car is an unadulterated threat to its occupants and everyone else on the road if it doesn't boast at least as much "Stop." One of the most important things you can do for your car's braking system—and for yourself—is conduct a thorough brake inspection every 10,000 miles. That amounts to about once a year.

A proper inspection will let you catch and fix minor problems before they become major safety hazards. And it can save you money, since problems may well result from a relatively insignificant condition—one you can correct without resorting to costly professional help.

The full inspection has two general parts. Begin with tests you run while the car sits in the driveway. You'll follow this with a road test. In each case, you will learn precisely what steps to take, what results to watch for, and how to interpret them.

In many cases, problems you discover can have any of a number of causes. For example, there are four major reasons your brake pedal might feel spongy. They range from air in the hydraulic system, requiring that you bleed it (easy enough) to drums worn so thin they must be replaced (also easy—but costly).

Whatever problem you're faced with, begin with the easiest, least expensive of the procedures called for. Proceed by steps to the more difficult, more expensive operations—hoping that you will have cured the problem early.

The chart shows eight different conditions you may find, and matches each with a group of possible causes.

Inspection in the driveway

Apply heavy foot pressure to the brake pedal (with the engine running at idle speed if you have a power brake system). The pedal should feel firm, not spongy or springy.

If it does feel spongy, however, check first to be sure the vent hole in the cover of the master cylinder isn't clogged. Remember that safety regulations require a dual master cylinder with one outlet feeding pressure to the front brakes, the other feeding the rear. (In some imports, the systems have been split diagonally—with the right-front and left-rear on one line. And there are even some in which one system feeds both rear brakes and one front-wheel brake while the other feeds the same rears and the other front.) Dual master cylinders have vent holes for each subsystem. There are two fluid reservoirs and two hydraulic pistons. They operate in tandem, controlled by a single push rod.

The usual cause of a spongy brake pedal is air trapped in the hydraulic system. Bleeding gets rid of this. Air can enter when the fluid level becomes low or a brake part is disconnected, then reinstalled.

A bleed screw is provided at each wheel cylinder. The order in which wheel cylinders are bled is of little importance, but be sure you hit all four of them.

Before you bleed a power brake system, purge the vacuum by depressing and releasing the brake pedal five or six times with the engine off.

Brake bleeding procedure

Here are the steps to follow in bleeding a hydraulic brake system:

1. If necessary, fill the master-cylinder fluid reservoir (both reservoirs if a dual system) with new brake fluid. After bleeding each cylinder, recheck the reservoir and keep the level within ¼ to ½ inch of the top.

2. Attach the bleeder hose, about 18 inches of vacuum hose, to the wheel-cylinder bleed screw. Submerge the other end in a container partly filled with brake fluid. A transparent container is best; you'll be watching for bubbles.

3. While a helper puts steady pressure on the brake pedal, open the bleed screw about ¾ turn. Pressure must be maintained until the screw is closed. When the fluid from the end of the hose stops bubbling, close the screw. Repeat the procedure at the other wheels.

Discard the old fluid. After bleeding the brakes, make sure the master cylinder is full.

Another cause of a spongy pedal is a soft or weak brake hose that expands under pressure. Feel hoses; they should be firm. If not, replace them.

After checking for a spongy pedal, observe pedal reserve. If the pedal is low, brakes probably need adjusting.

Checking self-adjusters

Brakes in cars built since the early 1960s are self-adjusting. Make several forward and reverse stops, coming to a complete stop every time. Pedal height should build up. If not, the linings are probably too badly worn to be adjusted or there is another problem. The self-adjusting mechanism may be in bad shape.

Now check for leaks in the hydraulic system by holding your foot lightly on the pedal for 15 seconds. There should be no pedal movement. The pedal should be just as firm when you try again, pressing down hard. If the car has power brakes, repeat the procedure with the engine running.

NEWER MASTER CYLINDERS have double reservoirs. Be sure the vent hole in each cover is clear to let atmospheric pressure keep brake lines full.

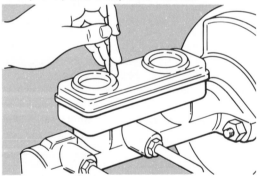

THE DIAPHRAGM covering the fluid reservoir of a dual master cylinder is marked "fluid side" and "cover side." Be sure the diaphragm is installed the right way.

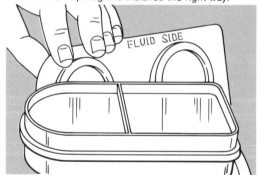

A PIECE OF VACUUM hose about 18 inches long helps in bleeding brakes. It's important that this hose fits snugly on the bleeder valves.

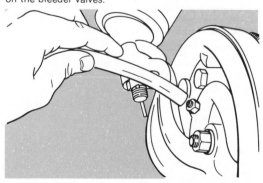

BE SURE RUBBER brake-fluid hose lines are tight, firm, clean, without cuts, cracks, or obvious leaks. Keep them clear of the running gear's moving parts.

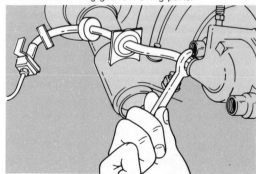

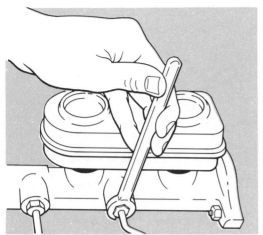

CHECK CONNECTIONS AT the master cylinder. All must be tight. Watch carefully for indications fluid has been leaking or that lines are vulnerable.

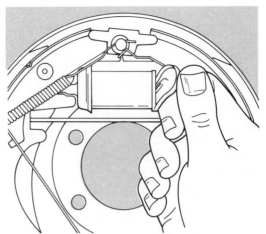

PEEL BACK BOTH boots when inspecting wheel cylinders. Leaks mean you lose fluid pressure and any fluid on the linings can destroy their braking effectiveness.

If the brake pedal gives way, there's a leak somewhere. Inspect the master cylinder first. Look for fluid around connections and see that the connections are tight.

Check all brake lines to each wheel for leaks. Try to tighten leaky connections before replacing hose. Make sure hoses and lines are free of dents, cracks, and cuts.

Wheel cylinders can also leak. You'll have to pull the wheels to check them. Peel back both boots of each cylinder. If fluid leaks, the cylinder must be rebuilt.

The master cylinder

If hoses, lines and wheel cylinders show no leaks, the fading brake pedal is caused by damage inside the master cylinder. Fluid may be leaking from around a secondary cup into the boot where you can't see it, although you may be able to detect the odor inside the car.

It isn't economically practical or 100-percent safe to rebuild a master cylinder, especially the newer, dual type. Besides the work involved, the necessary kit runs close to the cost of a new cylinder. Wheel cylinders are something else. It pays to rebuild them yourself.

Continue your driveway inspection by putting the car on jackstands or a lift (if you can talk a gas station operator out of the use of his). If you jack the car up, be sure to block the wheels still on the ground. Test the front wheels, then the rear. Release the parking brake and be sure each wheel spins freely without drag.

With light pressure on the pedal, all wheels should have similar drag as you spin them by hand.

If wheels don't revolve properly during this test, you probably have an inside problem with linings or cylinders. But if only the rear brakes drag, the parking brake may be hung up or adjusted too tightly. Release the lever. The cable should have some play. If not, adjustment or lubrication should cure the problem.

Finally, pull one of the front wheels and inspect brake linings. New linings are generally $3/16$ in. thick. Used linings should be no thinner than $1/16$ in. If you can't judge, use a gauge. If one set of linings is worn, replace them all.

Now for road testing

Putting a brake through its paces on the road tells how it's working under actual operating conditions. Pick a dry, clean, reasonably smooth and level road. And make sure tires are properly inflated.

Be careful not to fade brakes by overusing them during tests. If they do fade, let them cool for 10 minutes before proceeding.

The first test is at 10 to 15 mph. Make several stops, alternating between light and medium pedal applications. Come to a full stop each time.

Notice the effort required. Do brakes grab? Does the car pull? Is too much effort needed? If so, there's probably a problem with the linings, master or wheel cylinder(s), or drums.

Remember that conditions other than brakes can make the car pull. Loose or worn wheel bearings, loose steering, and maladjusted camber are all possibilities.

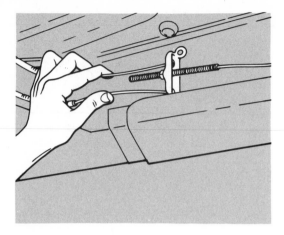

SOME SLACK is called for in the parking-brake cable. Otherwise that system may be constantly applied, making the brakes drag too much and wear too fast.

Diagnosis by sound

Open the windows, turn off any accessories, and listen. Try to tell the wheel that's generating a squeal, click, or scraping sound. Driving beside a wall makes noises more audible.

Speed up to 55 mph and make a few light-pedal stops. Is there chatter or shudder? If so, check for worn or loose wheel bearings. If the bearings are okay, suspect out-of-round drums.

From 55 mph, make several hard-pedal stops—as hard as you can without skidding. Come to a complete stop each time and drive at least two miles between stops to avoid overheating and fading the brakes. Listen for any unusual sound and check for undue effort in stopping.

You can make sure your car's "Stop" is at least as good as its "Go."

BRAKE DIAGNOSIS CHART

CONDITION	CAUSE
Low pedal (excessive pedal travel needed to apply brakes)	D E G K
Spongy pedal (a springy sensation of the pedal upon application)	G I J K
Hard pedal (excessive pedal pressure needed to stop the car)	D E H J K L
Fading pedal (pedal falls away under foot pressure)	G I J K L
Grabbing or pulling	B C E F G H J L M
Noise (squeal, click, scrape)	D E F G H
Chatter or shudder	B E G H
Dragging brakes	A D E F H J K L

KEY:

A—Parking brake improperly adjusted or sticking.
B—Loose wheel bearings.
C—Front-end misalignment or uneven tire tread.
D—Brake shoes improperly adjusted; automatic adjuster out of commission.
E—Worn, contaminated or distorted brake linings.
F—Weak or broken shoe return spring.
G—Cracked, thin, scored or out-of-round drums.
H—Brake support plate rusted, loose or worn.
I—Air in hydraulic system fluid.
J—Hoses and lines soft or weak, kinked, collapsed, dented, clogged, loosely connected, or leaking.
K—Damaged master cylinders.
L—Damaged wheel cylinder.
M—Check tire pressure.

PULL EITHER FRONT wheel to check linings, since they do most of the braking. Both sides wear essentially the same; if one is going, replace both or—all four.

CHECK THE LININGS at their thinnest point; at least 1/16 inch is necessary. Using a gauge is more reliable than measuring the thickness by eyeballing it.

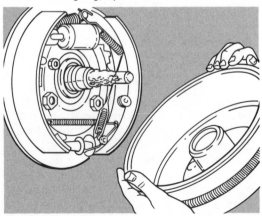

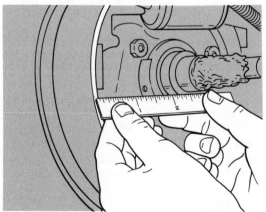

Drum brake system service

■ THERE'S A BIG saving in doing your own brake work. You will need some special tools you may not have, including:
- Drum-to-brake shoe clearance gauge
- Brake-cylinder clamps (4)
- Brake spring tools
- Brake bleeder wrench
- Adjusting tool
- Brake-drum micrometer

You don't have to buy a brake-drum micrometer if you get a brake shop to do your drum work. Shops charge per drum for milking and turning. You may also want to have a brake shop grind new brake linings to make full contact with drums, but this isn't always necessary since most high-quality linings are preground by the maker.

Major tasks involved in brake overhaul are (1) servicing brake drums; (2) replacing shoes and linings; (3) servicing wheel cylinders. The master cylinder will also require overhaul or replacing if it's leaking.

Removing brake drums

■ **To remove rear brake drums,** release the parking brake and relieve tension on the parking-brake cable. On most cars this is done by loosening or removing the adjusting nut at the equalizer (Drawing 1).

It might also be necessary to back off the brake-shoe adjusting mechanism before drums, front and rear, can be removed. On some cars, there is a slot in the backing plate through which this is done.

Remove the cover over the slot, insert a brake-adjusting tool and engage the teeth of the adjusting wheel (called a star wheel). Back off the star wheel until drag disappears. Be sure to reinstall the access hole cover (Drawing 2).

On other cars, access to the star wheel is gained through a lanced area in the brake drum. Knock out the plug in the lanced area. Insert the tool and proceed to disengage star wheel tension as just described.

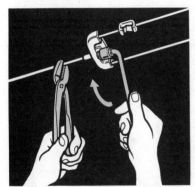

1. Parking-brake cable tension is released by loosening adjusting nut.

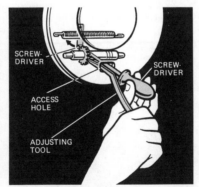

2. Adjusting tool is necessary to back off star wheel (except Wagner).

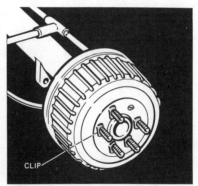

3. Rear-wheel drumclips (speed nuts) must be removed to remove drum.

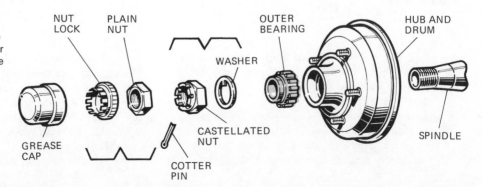

4. Typical front wheel bearing assembly is shown here. You'll have to disassemble the outer wheel bearing to remove drum. Take off grease cap, cotter pin, castellated nut (or plain nut and locknut), thrust washer and then outer wheel bearing.

NUT LOCK PLAIN NUT WASHER OUTER BEARING HUB AND DRUM CASTELLATED NUT GREASE CAP COTTER PIN SPINDLE

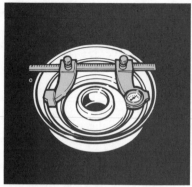

5. Brake drum is checked for wear, out-of-roundness and taper.

6. Lightly buff drums that are in good condition with emery cloth.

7. Use clamp to hold cylinder boots in place to prevent fluid leakage.

8. Remove anchor pins and take off the brake shoe return springs.

9. Hold-down springs are compressed and cups rotated to line up with pins.

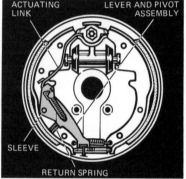

10. Self-adjusting mechanism for Delco-Moraine brakes is shown here.

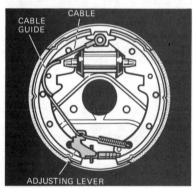

11. Self-adjusting mechanism for Bendix brakes is shown here.

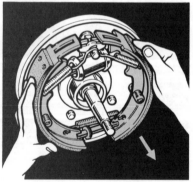

12. Brake shoes, adjusting screw and spring are removed.

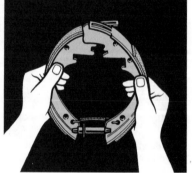

13. Separate shoes by relieving tension on the adjusting spring.

Remember: Before you finish the job, make sure you get new covers for lanced areas. Holes must be sealed to keep dirt and water from getting into the brake.

■ **If you are working on front wheel drum brakes,** in most cars you have to disassemble outer wheel bearings to remove drums. Take off the grease cap, cotter pin, castellated nut (or plain nut and locknut), thrust washer and outer wheel bearings (Drawing 3). Lay these parts on a clean surface.

■ **If you are overhauling rear wheel drum brakes,** take off the rear wheel and tire assembly. Metal clips (speed nuts) are probably holding the drum to the axle. Take off speed nuts and remove the drum (Drawing 4).

With drums off the vehicle, examine brake linings. Their condition can often tip you off to defective brake drums. Look for:

■ Linings serving one wheel that are worn down more than linings serving other wheels. The drum on that wheel is probably rough.

■ Uneven wear from side to side on any one set of linings. The drum is probably tapered.

■ Linings badly worn at toe or heel, indicating a drum out-of-round.

If compressed air is available, blow loose dirt from drums. If there is no compressed air, use a stiff bristle brush to remove dirt.

If drum has oil, grease or hardened dirt on it, wash it thoroughly with a nonoil-base cleaning solvent, such as carburetor cleaner or lacquer thinner. Check to see where oil or grease is coming from and make repairs before reinstalling drums. The leak likely is from a defective brake cylinder or front-wheel-hub grease seal.

Closely inspect each drum for cracks. A cracked brake drum should be replaced. Never attempt to weld it closed. This won't work and may lead to a serious accident.

■ **Even if drums look good,** with no indication of taper, out-of-roundness or damage, still have them checked with a micrometer for excessive wear (Drawing 5).

Take measurements at open and closed edges of the friction surface, and at right angles to each other. If taper or out-of-roundness exceeds .006 inch (.004 inch for Chrysler Total Contact brakes), the drum is not fit for use and should be turned.

If drums have to be turned to get them even and smooth, remove only enough metal to obtain a true surface. But keep in mind that if one drum has to be machined, the other drum on the same axle should be turned to the *same* diameter—even if it does not need machining—to assure braking equalization. For the same reason, if one brake drum has to be discarded, replace the other one on the same axle.

Every brake drum made since Dec. 31, 1970, has been stamped with a discard dimension. This is the permissible *wear* dimension, not the allowable turning dimension. If the drum cannot be turned so .030 inch is left for wear, replace the drum.

■ **If drums are true and smooth,** needing no turning, use some fine emery cloth to polish out slight score marks (Drawing 6). If this won't remove them, the drum should be turned.

Removing shoes and linings

The following step-by-step guide applies to drum brakes on most late-model cars. If your setup differs, the changes will be minor and you should be able to compensate using this outline:

1. Install brake-cylinder clamps to keep fluid from leaking (Drawing 7). Some brakes have brake-cylinder stops built into the backing plate, and need no clamps. In any event, don't press the brake pedal after shoe-return springs are removed.

2. Loosen the brake-spring anchor pin and remove the brake-shoe return springs (Drawing 8). Your set-up may not have springs attached directly to the anchor pin. They may be hooked to a plate that, in turn, is held by an anchor pin. Whatever, examine the arrangement closely before proceeding. Be sure the layout is firmly in mind (make notes and a sketch, if necessary) so springs may be reinstalled properly.

3. Remove shoe-retaining parts. There are differences from brake to brake. Some use a coil spring-cup-pin arrangement (Drawing 9). Others have pins with the outside end retained by a spring clip. Still others use tension hold-down springs, enlarged on one end and with a hook on the other that engages a retainer through the backing plate.

4. Remove self-adjusting parts. On Delco Moraine brakes, you must lift off actuating link, lever and pivot assembly, sleeve and return spring (Drawing 10). Discard damaged parts.

On Bendix brakes (Drawing 11), slip the adjusting cable off the anchor pin and unhook bottom end of the adjusting lever. Remove cable guide, but don't remove the adjusting lever yet. It's easier to get it off after shoes are removed.

On Wagner brakes, remove screw holding the adjusting crank, lift off crank and unhook adjusting links from the anchor pin and adjusting lever. Wait until you have taken off brake shoes to remove adjusting lever.

5. On rear brakes, remove the parking brake strut by spreading shoes apart slightly. Disconnect the parking brake lever, which may be held either by a retaining clip or bolt, or may be hooked in place.

6. If anchor plate is used, slip it off anchor pin; if plate is bolted on, leave it be.

7. Spread brake-shoe anchor ends and take shoes off brake-cylinder links. Remove shoes, and adjusting screw and spring as an assembly (Drawing 12). Some brakes don't have brake cylinder links. Shoes ride directly on brake cylinder pistons.

8. To separate shoes, relieve adjusting spring tension by overlapping anchor ends of shoes

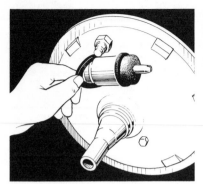

14. Brake cylinder at each wheel should be checked for leaks.

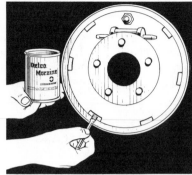

15. Pads on which shoes rest are lubricated to prevent noise and wear.

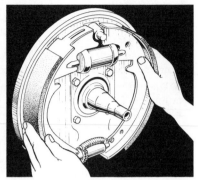

16. New shoes, with adjusting mechanism and spring, are installed.

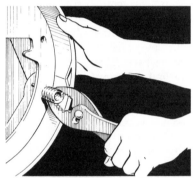

17. Hold-down pins that retain the brake shoe get a quarter turn.

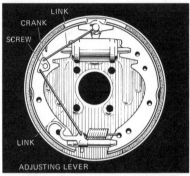

18. Delco-Moraine self-adjusting mechanism is shown here installed.

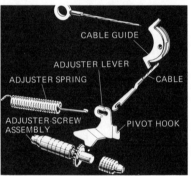

19. On Bendix unit, self-adjusting mechanism uses components shown.

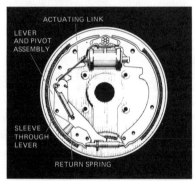

20. On Wagner unit, reassemble self-adjusting mechanism as shown above.

21. Drum-to-brake-shoe clearance gauge measures inside diameter.

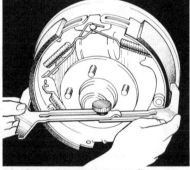

22. Gauge is turned over to fit over shoes. Expand linings to meet gauge.

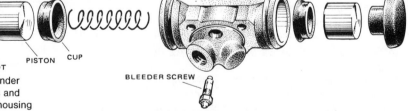

EXPLODED VIEW 1: Typical brake cylinder (wheel cylinder) has two boots, pistons and cups, plus a common spring, cylinder housing and bleeder screw.

EXPLODED VIEW 2: Typical adjusting mechanism (less levers and cables) should be disassembled, cleaned and inspected; adjusting screw should be lubricated.

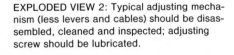
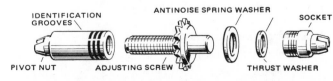

(Drawing 13). Unhook spring; remove adjusting screw. Parts are now separated.

Take a close look at your wheel cylinders while other brake parts are removed from the backing plate. Inspect boots for cuts, tears and cracks. Physical damage indicates a need for cylinder overhaul.

■ **If the cylinder has external (rubber) boots, as most do, carefully pull back the lower edge of the boot as shown in Drawing 14.** If more than a drop of fluid spills out, the cylinder is damaged and should be overhauled or replaced. Each cylinder has two boots. Be sure to check both ends.

Some brake cylinders have metal caps. To check such cylinders for damage, you have to remove either the connecting link or cap on one end of the cylinder. If fluid runs out, overhaul or replace the cylinder.

Brake cylinders

Here's how to service brake cylinders that need repair:

1. From behind the backing plate, clean away dirt around the connection and disconnect the brake line from the cylinder. Tape the open end of line to keep fluid from leaking and to keep dirt out.

2. If links are used between cylinder and brake shoes, remove them. Now, pull off external (rubber) boots with pliers and discard them. Remove metal caps used instead of boots.

3. Remove pistons, cups and spring assembly as shown in exploded view 1. (Note how they come out, so that, later, you can replace them in the right way.) While removing the spring assembly, be careful not to scratch the bore of the cylinder. Also remove bleeder screw from the cylinder and make sure passages are clear.

4. Examine the cylinder bore. If it is just stained or discolored, the cylinder can be kept in use. If bore is scratched or corroded, replace cylinder with a new one.

Important: Don't confuse staining with corrosion. Pit marks or roughness in the bore indicate corrosion.

5. Remove stains and discoloration with crocus cloth wrapped around your finger. *Revolve the cylinder* on the crocus cloth. Do not slide the cloth lengthwise through the cylinder. You may scratch the bore.

6. Wash the cylinder in clean brake fluid, shake off excess, and allow the part to air dry. Do not use a rag to dry the cylinder. Lint can get on the bore surface.

7. A brake cylinder rebuild kit is needed at this point. All rubber parts are contained in such a kit. However, metal parts such as pistons may not be included in the kit. If not, clean used parts in clean brake fluid and let them dry before reuse. If pistons are damaged, and you can't get replacements, you will have to replace the whole cylinder.

8. Inspect the bleeder screw and bleeder screw inlet hole for stripped threads. Replace a damaged screw.

9. Lubricate the bore with clean brake fluid before putting parts in the cylinder (be sure your hands are clean). Insert the spring assembly and new cups. See that cups go in the right way. Recall how they came out. Usually, the flat surface goes to the outer end of the cylinder.

10. Insert pistons properly. They must go back in the same position they were when they came out of the bore. Normally, pistons are installed with their flat surfaces toward the center of the cylinder.

11. Press new boots into place and install links, if they are used. Boots must be seated firmly.

12. Place the cylinder back on the brake backing plate and tighten bolts. Hook up the brake line.

Backing Plate

■ **Turn your attention to the backing plate.** If you have compressed air available, blow off loose dirt. Use a wire brush to loosen caked-on deposits and scale. If there is no compressed air, use a wire brush only.

Check backing plate for minor surface defects, such as corrosion. Fine emery cloth will remove this.

Examine the backing plate. If it's cracked or bent, it must be replaced.

Apply a thin film of brake lubricant to the raised pads on the backing plate (Drawing 15). On these pads the new shoes will rest.

Self-adjust mechanism

Disassemble the adjusting mechanism at your workbench and clean the parts (see exploded view 2). Make sure the adjusting screw threads fully in the pivot nut without binding, and that no adjusting teeth are damaged. Discard bad parts.

Lubricate the adjusting screw and reassemble adjusting mechanism.

Reassembly

At this point you can install new shoes and replace all other parts, but first there are a couple of points that needed emphasis:

Important: Depending on the final diameter of brake drums (if they have been turned), you may have to use oversize replacement brake shoes and linings. Generally, if a drum is turned from .060-inch oversize to maximum discard dimension, .030-inch oversize linings are used, but check your parts man to see what's recommended for your particular brake.

1. When you have drums miked and turned, have the brake shop match each new lining to its respective drum by grinding it to the drum's micrometer reading. This eliminates high spots and assures linings will make full contact with drums. However, high-quality brake linings are generally preground by the maker, so this may not be necessary.

2. In the case of Bendix brakes, hook the adjusting lever into the hole in the secondary shoe web. Wagner self-adjusting brakes should have the adjusting lever placed in the secondary shoe web with the slot in the lever engaging to the full depth with the slot in the shoe web.

3. Lay brake shoes on a clean surface in correct mounting position. Connect the lower spring between the shoes. On Bendix brakes, the spring is connected between the primary shoe and adjusting lever. Engage the adjusting mechanism.

4. Carry the assembly to the car and place it on the brake backing plate, engaging the brake cylinder (Drawing 16). Position the shoes' webs on the anchoring unit.

5. On rear brakes, spread shoes slightly, reinstall parking-brake strut and springs and rejoin parking-brake lever to the secondary shoe.

6. On all brakes except Delco-Moraine, reinstall the shoe retaining parts. On Delco, do this after installing the rest of the self-adjusting mechanism.

On units with hold-down springs, push the hold-down pin through the backing plate and shoe, and hold pin in place. Grasp the hold-down spring and cup with pliers, place the spring on the pin, and give the pin a quarter turn to lock it in place (Drawing 17). If spring clips are used, compress the clip and snap it in place on the pin.

If brake hold-down devices are tension-type retaining pins, fit the spring-retaining clip through the backing plate and use a small punch to extend the spring, hooking it on to the retaining clip.

7. Install the rest of the self-adjusting unit as follows:

On Delco-Moraine brakes (Drawing 18), hook one end of the actuating link over the anchor pin or on the anchor plate if plate is bolted on. Hook the other end to the lever and pivot assembly. Position the lever on the secondary shoe, placing the lever return spring between the lever and shoe. Install the sleeve, then the hold-down parts.

On Bendix brakes (Drawing 19), install the cable guide on the secondary shoe, hook one end of the cable on the actuating lever, run the cable around the guide, and slip the cable eye over the anchor pin.

On Wagner brakes (Drawing 20), bolt the crank to the secondary shoe. Install offset ends of the links onto the crank holes. Hook upper link over the top groove in the anchor pin. Lift the adjusting lever slightly, and hook bottom link to the lever.

Important: Defer installation of the upper link until you install shoe return springs since it is installed on the anchor pin *over* the spring.

8. Install shoe return springs. Hook springs to shoes first and then attach them to the anchor assembly using a spring installation tool. Spring installation varies, so examine springs before removing them.

● **To finish your brake job,** use a drum-to-brake shoe clearance gauge to check drum's inside diameter. Tighten the lock screw (Drawing 21).

Turn the tool over and fit it over the brake shoes. You will probably have to expand the shoes manually by turning the star wheel to get the linings to extend to the gauge. The gauge should just slide over the linings. That's a proper fit (Drawing 22).

Reinstall brake drums and tighten the parking-brake equalizer until there is tension on brake cables.

Before moving the car, check for ample brake pedal. Now drive the car forward about 200 feet, stop, then back up 200 feet. Do this a few times, coming to a complete halt each time.

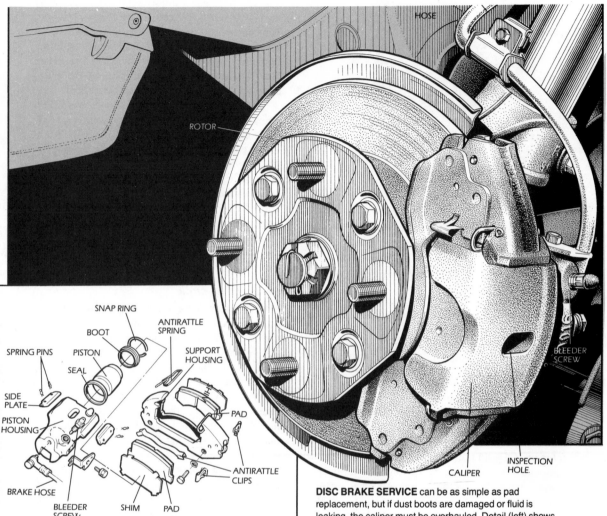

DISC BRAKE SERVICE can be as simple as pad replacement, but if dust boots are damaged or fluid is leaking, the caliper must be overhauled. Detail (left) shows all parts of typical caliper.

Servicing disc brakes

■ MOST OF THE routine service on disc brakes is a do-it-yourself job. You can certainly replace linings (pads)—plus the shims and antirattle springs or clips that may be attached to pads. You can probably rebuild calipers, too. If a caliper has to be replaced—another job you can do yourself.

It's when you get into disc brake *overhaul* that you'll need some professional help. For rotor work, for example, you'll need measuring instru-

ments (a micrometer and dial gauge) and a rotor machining tool. Rather than make such an investment, most of us will admit the limitations of a home garage and pay to have the work done.

Before you start brake work it's suggested that you have the factory service manual or general auto repair manual for specific instructions, and specs for your car.

When is overhaul needed?

There are two ways to determine if disc brakes need repair before the linings are worn enough to cause extensive rotor damage. Brakes in Ford and GM cars and light trucks manufactured since the early 70's have pad-wear sensors. When a lining gets to within .03 inch of the rivet heads, this spring-steel sensor comes in contact with the rotor and a high-frequency squeak is emitted. The warning sound continues until the brakes are

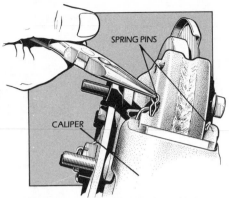

1 Two spring pins in each slide plate must be removed to release the caliper.

applied and the sound changes pitch or ceases.

If the warning is ignored, wear progresses, but the raucous sound eventually ceases. By then, it's probably too late to save the rotor from extensive damage.

If your vehicle is a Chrysler model, it probably doesn't have wear sensors. Most imported cars don't have wear-sensor-equipped disc brakes either, although they have begun to appear on some of the newest models.

Checking wear visually

To find out if a vehicle without wear sensors requires pad replacement, remove the wheels and calipers and take out the pads to check the amount of friction material remaining. Nonmetallic pads should not be allowed to wear beyond the point where 1/16 inch of friction material protrudes above the rivets. Semimetallic pads can wear to within 1/32 inch of the rivets. If the pads are not riveted to the backing plates, the amount of friction material should equal the thickness of the backing plates.

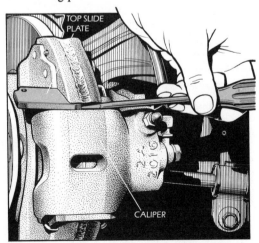

2 After the spring pins are removed, tap the top and bottom slide plates out sideways to disengage caliper.

If you have a late-model import vehicle, it may have a swivel-mount caliper. By removing a bolt, you can swivel the head of the caliper away from the main body. You can then measure the lining thickness without removing the pads. The swivel head also makes it easier to replace the pads, since you don't have to remove the caliper.

Inspect nonsensor-equipped pads at 30,000 miles. If they're okay, check them every 15,000 miles until they need replacing.

Most calipers equipped with nonsensor-type pads have inspection holes that let you view one or both linings, so you can judge the extent of wear without disassembling everything—if you know for certain that your pads are bonded to the backing plates and do not have rivets. *Caution:* To inspect and overhaul front-disc brakes, have the vehicle resting on jackstands with the rear wheels blocked.

Metal or phenolic

Let's review some things you should know in order to remove pads for inspection and replacement. This discussion will deal only with single-piston disc brakes. They've been used on most cars since 1970.

The piston in the caliper, which is activated hydraulically and presses pads against the rotor when you step on the brake pedal, is made of nickel chrome-plated steel or plastic (a phenolic material similar in hardness and smoothness to Bakelite).

Introduced around 1975, phenolic pistons have been increasing in popularity. They weigh less, are less expensive and provide better insulation than metal, thus protecting brake fluid from heat generated by metallic disc pads. And they don't corrode as metal pistons can. However, phenolic

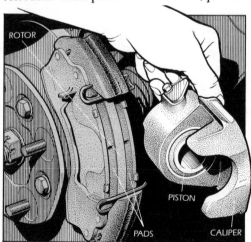

3 When caliper is removed, don't let it hang by the brake hose. Support it with a wire hooked to the chassis.

pistons have to be treated more gently than metal because they can crack and chip.

You can't easily distinguish piston composition with the disc brake unit assembled. So treat pistons as if they are phenolic unless you are certain that they aren't.

Retracting pistons

The caution to take is simple enough. When pushing the piston back into its bore, don't slip a screwdriver or pry bar under the pad so it's directly on a piston.

You have to push the piston into its bore to free the pads on GM vehicles. To do this, place a C-clamp so the flat on the end of the screw rests on the pad, and the stationary part of the clamp rests on the rear of the caliper. Tighten the clamp to push the piston back into its bore just enough for the pads to clear the rotor.

On Ford calipers, you'll need a ¾ × 1 × 2¾-inch block of wood to retract the piston once the caliper is off.

Note: Even if the piston is metal, it's not wise to push it back with a screwdriver. You might nick the plating.

Before pushing the piston into the bore, drain about half the fluid from the master cylinder. Discard it and have a *sealed* container of fresh brake fluid ready to add to the master cylinder when the job is done. Buy the brand of fluid recommended by the carmaker or another high-quality replacement that conforms to Department of Transportation (DOT) specification 3, 4 or 5. Fluids may not mix chemically, especially the glycol base DOT 3 and 4 fluids if they are mixed with the silicone-base DOT 5 fluid.

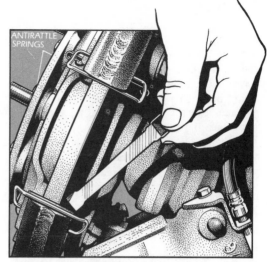

4 Clips that hold antirattle springs may require replacement. If so, they'll be supplied in the pad kit.

Bolts or plates

Most carmakers secure calipers to their supports in one of two ways: with bolts or with pin-held retaining plates.

If the calipers on your disc brakes use bolts, push the piston back into the bore and see if the bolts are fastened on the outboard end of the caliper with retaining clips. If so, pull them off. The outboard end of the caliper is the side resting on the outside surface of the rotor.

Determine how to remove the bolts. Those that have hex or Allen heads should be unscrewed with the appropriate wrench. Other bolts may be tapped out with a hammer and drift. These are the ones usually retained by clips.

If there are no bolts, the caliper is probably being retained at the top and bottom by slide plates. Look for spring pins holding these plates. There are probably four of them—two holding the top slide plate and two holding the bottom plate. Pull the pin out and save them (see Fig. 1).

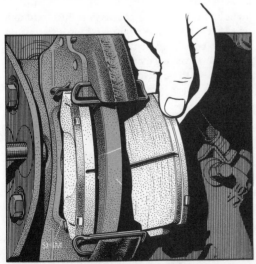

5 Before removing pads, sketch the exact position of all shims, hardware, retaining clips and springs.

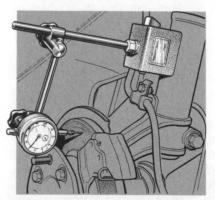

6 Rotor runout can be checked with a dial indicator while spinning the rotor by hand.

Then, tap out the top and bottom slide plates (Fig. 2).

Many Ford and AMC calipers are retained on their machined guides by a support key and screw. After removing the screw, drive the key out of the anchor with a hammer and drift.

Again, check a service manual for specific instructions. If you're still not sure how to do the job, get professional help. Don't take chances when it comes to brake work.

When the bolts or slide plates have been removed, lift the caliper off the rotor (Fig. 3). You may have to push the caliper down and then pull it away from the rotor so it clears the antirattle springs. With some setups, you don't have to replace the antirattle springs. However, they may be held by clips that often have to be replaced (Fig. 4).

The best way to know which parts to replace and which to retain is by purchasing a brake pad kit for your particular vehicle. It will contain pads and all of the hardware that should be replaced when doing an overhaul. It also provides installation and lubrication instructions.

Caliper care

If you're only replacing pads and hardware, you don't have to disconnect the brake hose from the caliper. However, if you do remove the caliper, don't let it hang by the brake hose, which can split under the weight. Fashion a hook from a wire coat hanger, slip one end into one of the caliper bolt holes and hang the caliper on a part of the chassis.

Pads are held in calipers by support springs, retaining clips or retaining pins. They may also have shims (Fig. 5). Before removing pieces of hardware, make a note or sketch of how they lie in relation to the pads. Then, take the old pads off and throw them away.

Check around the piston bore for signs of moisture, which indicate that fluid is leaking. Also, inspect the dust boot for cracks and cuts. If leaks are present or the boot is damaged, overhaul or replace the caliper.

Overhauling a caliper

Calipers have a small square-cut rubber O-ring that helps draw the piston back away from the pads when pressure on the brake pedal is released. If this O-ring loses elasticity, which it will in time, the piston won't draw back and the pads won't release. The result will be slight pad-to-rotor contact and premature pad wear, noise, fading and/or uneven braking. For this reason it is wise, though not essential, to overhaul a caliper when replacing pads.

Now the question arises: Should you overhaul the calipers yourself, replace them with rebuilt units or turn the job over to a pro? The least expensive approach is to overhaul them yourself. The next in line, costwise, is to install rebuilt calipers, which you can buy from an auto parts dealer. Obviously, a pro is going to be the most expensive.

Overhaul procedures

Here's a general idea of the overhauling procedure to help you decide whether you want to tackle the job. If you do it yourself, make sure you have specific instructions for your vehicle.

Note: If one caliper has to be overhauled or replaced, the caliper on the other side should also be overhauled or replaced. Also, when replacing pads, replace them on both sides of the car.

1. After removing the caliper from the rotor, keep the caliper on the car with the brake hose attached. Place a rag in the caliper to catch the piston and brake fluid. Make sure no one is near the car and carefully push on the brake pedal to ease the piston out of the bore. Don't get brake fluid on your car's fender—it will take off the paint.

This is a reasonably safe way to remove a piston and is recommended if calipers have phenolic pistons. If a caliper is already off the vehicle and has a metal piston, you can apply spurts of compressed air through the bleed screw to ease out the piston. Place a shop rag in the caliper to catch the piston and keep your fingers clear.

Much greater air pressure might be needed to get out a phenolic piston, but it could expel the piston with such force that it would be destroyed or else injure anyone in its way. To remove a phenolic piston from a caliper, it's best to attach the caliper to the brake hose and force the piston from the bore using hydraulic pressure.

In a few cars—Toyota Supra, for example—pistons have to be unscrewed using a special tool.

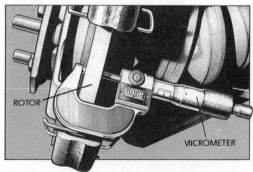

7 Check rotor parallelism by taking measurements on the circumference. Machine rotor if it doesn't meet specs.

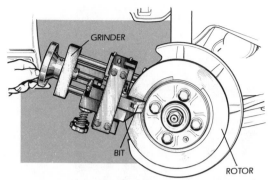

8 On-the-car rotor grinding is required on some models, notably Hondas, to get vibration-free brake operation.

They cannot be removed by applying hydraulic or air pressure.

2. Remove the caliper. When you disconnect the brake hose, cap it to prevent fluid loss.

3. Open the bleed screw to drain brake fluid. Remove the bleed screw and clean or replace it.

4. Remove the dust boot, following the manufacturer's instructions. Some dust boots are difficult to reinstall without special tools. In all cases, the dust boot must be replaced.

5. The rubber O-ring is more difficult to remove. Use a pointed wooden or plastic stick—a toothpick might work—to pry the seal out of the bore. Then, discard it.

Do not use a screwdriver or any other metal tool. You may scratch the bore or cause a burred edge on the O-ring groove and ruin the caliper.

6. Wash the caliper, bore and piston with denatured alcohol or clean brake fluid. Don't use kerosene, gasoline or any petroleum solvent. Residue left by these fluids can cause rubber brake parts to deteriorate.

Dry parts with a clean, lint-free cloth and an air hose aimed at the bore and other passages. If you don't have a compressor, let parts air-dry.

7. Examine the piston. If it is metal and is rusted, pitted or scored, throw it away. If it's phenolic and chipped or cracked, get rid of it, too.

Don't try to polish a metal piston. Any attempt to sand or buff away damage will destroy the plating.

8. Examine the bore. If it's scored or corroded, replace the caliper. But if it's only slightly stained, clean it by rotating a piece of crocus cloth, by hand, in the bore. Don't use a lot of pressure, and make sure you polish the bore all the way around. Don't slide the abrasive in and out, and don't use any abrasive except crocus cloth.

Incidentally, black stains on the bore wall are not something to get alarmed over. They're caused by the O-ring seal and aren't harmful.

9. Reinstall the bleed screw and lubricate a new O-ring with clean brake fluid. Push the O-ring into place at one spot in the groove and then gently work it inch-by-inch into the groove with your fingers. Make sure you don't twist the O-ring.

10. After lubricating both parts, start the piston into the bore. You may have to fit the dust boot over the piston before pushing it in all the way. Check your service manual instructions. If you need a special tool for dust boot installation, it's probably available at the parts store where you bought the pads.

11. After the new pads and caliper are in place, bleed the brake system.

Rotor service

Don't be misled by the fact that the rotors may look perfect. True, they might not be scored, but thickness variation (parallelism) and runout may be such that failure to catch something now will mean a problem like vibration or chatter later. You can't detect excessive parallelism or runout by eye. Measuring instruments are needed.

To find the extent of runout a pro will mount a dial indicator and slowly rotate the rotor, taking readings at several points (Fig. 6). He should also check parallelism by placing a micrometer at four or more points around the circumference of the rotor, each the same distance in from the edge of the rotor (Fig. 7). The findings should be checked against the manufacturer's allowable specification for the car. If the rotor fails to meet the spec, it will be machined.

When it comes to machining rotors, make sure your brake shop is aware of the latest technology. Rotors can be machined off the car on a brake lathe or on the car by using a special grinder. Some manufacturers—Honda, for one—require on-the-car grinding, since near-perfect parallelism is obtained with this equipment. Honda finds this necessary to eliminate a vibration that faulty parallelism causes.

When using an on-the-car grinder on a front-wheel-drive car, the transmission is placed in THIRD gear or D after the grinder is attached and the rotating rotor turns against the grinder's machining bits. If the car has rear-wheel drive, a drive mechanism is used to turn the rotors.

Obviously, if you have a car equipped with rotors that *must* be ground on a car, let a pro handle the entire brake job. After machining a rotor, a pro should remeasure it to make sure grinding hasn't removed metal beyond the minimum dimension stamped on the rotor by the manufacturer. If the rotor is too thin, you must replace it.

Butcher block made the expert way

■ BUTCHER BLOCKS are now enjoying a renaissance. These attractive hardwood surfaces are durable, versatile and easy to make.

Butcher blocks are most commonly used for active work surfaces such as kitchen countertops,

DOWEL PINS. Fluted dowel pins are used to join lengths of ¾ x 2-in. cherry. Note that they're joined in pairs first. Cross-section (top) reveals dowel locations.

THROUGH-BOLT. For the strongest butcher block joint, bolt each part together with a threaded rod. Counterbore end pieces (top) to accept a nut, washer and plug.

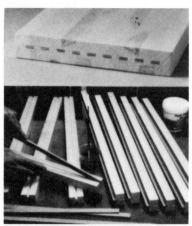

SPLINE JOINT. Assemble spline joints using mahogany plywood splines. Groove each member on both sides, except the end pieces (top), to accept the splines.

NAIL PINS. Cut pins from finishing nails using a pair of end-cut nippers. The pins strengthen the glued joint and prevent the wood from slipping when clamped.

GLUE JOINT. Use a glue-joint bit to cut mating edges on all parts. Then glue the parts at a plywood base. Crosssection (top) shows the tight-fitting joints.

DIRECT NAILING. Here's a quick and easy way to make a strong joint. Simply glue and nail one board to the next until the desired width butcher block top is formed.

PARQUET FLOORING. Glue hardwood flooring to a plywood base. After assembly, add trim around the butcher block to conceal the plywood edge (top).

chopping blocks and workbenches. The warm, hand-crafted look of butcher blocks also makes them a popular choice for furniture. Virtually any hardwood can be used to make butcher blocks, either alone or in combination with other species for a contrasting appearance.

These butcher block techniques are described: dowel pins, through-bolt, spline-joint, nail pins, glue-joint, direct-nailing and a top made using teak parquet flooring. Each technique provides an easy way to assemble strong, durable butcher block tops. The particular technique you choose depends on the size and function of the butcher block, the tools you have available and the desired finished appearance. For example, the through-bolt technique provides the strongest top and is recommended for large surfaces subjected to heavy poundings. If thin boards are used to make a smaller butcher block top, try the easy, direct-nailing method. In most situations, many of the techniques shown would be suitable.

Assembly

After milling the butcher block pieces to the same width and thickness, cut them ½ in. longer than needed to allow for final trimming with a portable circular saw or radial-arm saw. Next, arrange the pieces with the best side up. Then orient the pieces so that the wood grain of each piece is pointing in the same direction. Mark an arrow on each piece to indicate the grain direction. By pointing the grain in the same direction, the plane won't gouge the wood.

Now mark each board with a number or letter to help you arrange them for final assembly and to assure that you machine each piece from the same face or edge. This is especially important for techniques that require boring holes or cutting grooves.

Since most butcher block surfaces are exposed to water, use a water-resistant glue during assembly, such as plastic resin. Simply mix the powdered resin with water as per label instructions. Use a miniature paint roller to apply the glue evenly and quickly.

After planing and sanding the assembled top smooth, apply several coats of mineral oil or a non-toxic sealer.

IF YOU DON'T OWN a drill press, use a portable drill with a doweling jig to bore dowel pin holes. Note depth-stop collar on the drill bit.

APPLY GLUE to the walls of the holes and then tap in the pins using a wooden or plastic mallet so you don't damage the ends.

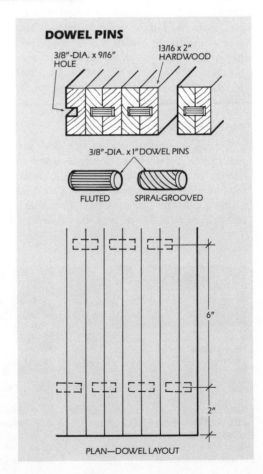

DOWEL PINS

3/8"-DIA. x 9/16" HOLE

13/16 x 2" HARDWOOD

3/8"-DIA. x 1" DOWEL PINS

FLUTED   SPIRAL-GROOVED

6"

2"

PLAN—DOWEL LAYOUT

Dowel pins

This technique uses hardwood dowel pins to join the butcher block members. The wood members are first joined in pairs, and then into blocks of four using a staggered dowel pattern. Continue joining the pieces this way until the desired width butcher block is obtained. It's important to use only fluted or spiral-grooved dowel pins, not sections or ordinary hardwood dowels. The flutes and spirals cut into the pins allow excess glue to escape the dowel hole during clamping. Otherwise, clamping pressure may cause the trapped glue to split the wood.

First, lay the butcher block members edge-to-edge on a flat surface. Then, using a framing square or T-square, draw centerlines for the first set of dowel holes every 6 in. Be sure to code each board with a number or letter to aid the final assembly.

Next, bore the dowel holes using a drill press or a portable drill with a doweling jig. Note that for a 1-in.-long dowel pin you must bore a 9/16-in.-deep hole in each board. The extra 1/16 in. retains a small amount of glue, just enough to make a strong joint. During assembly, be certain to apply glue to the walls of the dowel holes and along the faces of the mating boards. Clamp the pieces with bar or pipe clamps placed under and over the butcher block to prevent bowing. Be certain to scrape off hardening glue squeezed out before planing and sanding.

Through-bolt

When you're building a butcher block surface that's going to get a lot of abuse, such as a workbench, the through-bolt technique shown here is the one to use. The wood members are held together solidly by threaded steel rods that pass through holes bored in each board. Space the rods between 12 and 16 in. apart, depending on the size of the butcher block. For very wide butcher blocks, you can save money by using plain steel rod and threading the ends yourself.

Start by carefully center-boring holes in each piece using a drill press and fence. If the holes don't align the error will produce an uneven butcher block top. Next, counterbore the two boards to receive the washer, nut and wood plug. Then continue boring through the end pieces for the rod.

Glue and stack all the pieces and insert the rods through the holes with a nut and washer on one end. Position the last end piece and add the washer and nut. Tighten each rod little by little until the wood joints are closed tight. Finally, glue the wood plugs in place and sand them flush.

Spline joint

The spline-reinforced joint is one of the easiest to cut and assemble, yet it produces one of the strongest butcher blocks. Note that 1/4-in. mahogany plywood is used for the splines because the inner plies run crosswise and resist splitting.

Start by cutting 3/8-in.-deep grooves in both sides of each board using a 1/4-in.-wide dado blade on a table saw. Don't be concerned with cutting grooves in the *exact* center of the piece. It's more important to keep the same face of the piece against the saw fence when cutting both grooves. Simply flip the piece end for end so the grooves will match, centered or not.

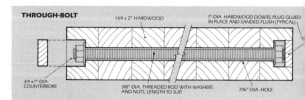

THROUGH-BOLT · 1-1/4 x 2" HARDWOOD · 1"-DIA. HARDWOOD DOWEL PLUG GLUED IN PLACE AND SANDED FLUSH (TYPICAL) · 3/4 x 1"-DIA. COUNTERBORE · 3/8"-DIA. THREADED ROD WITH WASHERS AND NUTS; LENGTH TO SUIT · 7/16"-DIA. HOLE

USE A SMALL PAINT ROLLER to spread the glue quickly and evenly. Glue and stack all pieces and then insert threaded rods.

USE TWO SOCKET WRENCHES to draw the joints closed. Mark the threads on one end to prevent the nut from running off.

There are two ways to assemble spline-joint butcher blocks. Glue the splines into one side of all the pieces and then assemble the top, or build up the butcher block progressively by adding one board and spline at a time.

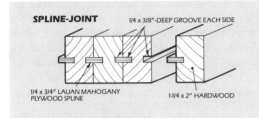

SPLINE-JOINT
1/4 x 3/8"-DEEP GROOVE EACH SIDE
1/4 x 3/4" LAUAN MAHOGANY PLYWOOD SPLINE
1-1/4 x 2" HARDWOOD

CUT the spline grooves on a table saw. Feather-board applies side pressure.

SPLINES are visible on end grain.

Nail pins

Short sections of finishing nails are used to align the boards of the butcher block and prevent slippage during gluing and clamping.

Bore a hole near each end on one side of every board. Then insert a nail pin, blunt end first, into each hole. Clamp the pieces together so the pin points make indentation marks. Unclamp the assembly, apply glue and reclamp, driving the pins in fully.

USE BAR CLAMPS to drive nail pins into adjacent pieces. Note board clamped across the top to keep the butcher block flat and even.

Glue joint

This tight-fitting joint is made with a glue-joint cutter on a shaper or on a table saw with a glue-joint molding cutter head. Note that a ¾-in. plywood base supports the butcher block.

Carefully adjust the cutter so that it's centered on the work piece edge. Next, shape the edges of each board. Assemble the butcher block onto the base with glue, then nail through the plywood and into the wood members. Add 1½-in.-wide trim around the butcher block to conceal the plywood edge.

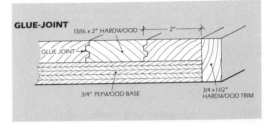

GLUE-JOINT
13/16 x 2" HARDWOOD
2"
GLUE JOINT
3/4" PLYWOOD BASE
3/4 x 1-1/2" HARDWOOD TRIM

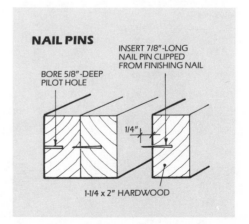

CUT THE TIGHT-FITTING GLUE JOINT on a shaper. Glue-joint molding cutter heads are also available for a table saw.

NAIL PINS
BORE 5/8"-DEEP PILOT HOLE
INSERT 7/8"-LONG NAIL PIN CLIPPED FROM FINISHING NAIL
1/4"
1-1/4 x 2" HARDWOOD

Direct nailing

The direct-nailing technique is used when making butcher blocks from boards less than 1 in. thick. Bore pilot holes in each board about 6 in. apart. Then glue and nail one board to the next using 1¼-in. finishing nails. Be sure to stagger the nails so you don't strike a nail in the preceding board. Finally, clamp the assembled butcher block until the glue dries.

Parquet flooring

Hardwood parquet flooring is available in a wide variety of patterns and wood species and makes attractive butcher blocks. Since most parquet flooring is only ¼ or ⅜ in. thick, a base is needed to support the butcher block. Make the base from two pieces of ¾-in. plywood. Glue the parquet to the plywood base with flooring adhesive. If teak parquet is used, as shown here, be sure to use an adhesive formulated specifically for teak, which is very oily. Complete the top by nailing on ½ x 1¾-in.-wide hardwood trim to conceal the plywood edge.

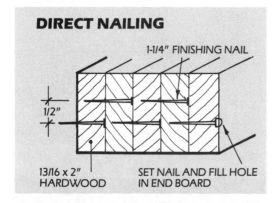

DIRECT NAILING

1-1/4" FINISHING NAIL

1/2"

13/16 x 2" HARDWOOD

SET NAIL AND FILL HOLE IN END BOARD

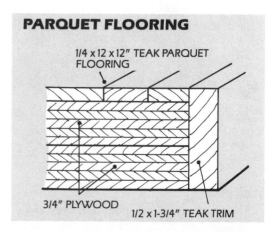

PARQUET FLOORING

1/4 x 12 x 12" TEAK PARQUET FLOORING

3/4" PLYWOOD

1/2 x 1-3/4" TEAK TRIM

DIRECT-NAILING technique is a quick and easy way to make a butcher block. Be certain to bore nail pilot holes first.

GLUE PARQUET FLOORING to a plywood base using the appropriate adhesive. Add a second plywood base for additional support.

Butcher block you can build

■ REGULAR BUTCHER BLOCKS are true heavyweights with solid maple tops from 12 to 18 in. thick. Those sold for home use average about 10 in. thick. Some have solid tops; many are simply thin shells as little as 1¼ in. thick. The one shown here is 2⅝ in. thick and uses poplar throughout instead of the traditional maple in the interest of economy and ease of fabrication. While poplar is considered a soft hardwood, it has sufficiently hard end grain.

Start by selecting kiln-dry lumber which is sound and absolutely warp-free. You'll need 50 ft. of ⁸/₄ by 4 in. for the top and 18 ft. of ¹⁰/₄ x 4¼ in. for gluing up the turning blocks for the legs. The dressed ⁸/₄ stock will normally measure 1¹³/₁₆ in. thick so that's the reason for the odd dimension of the blocks. The ¹⁰/₄ stock is necessary for the legs in order to permit dressing to a full 4-in. square after gluing.

ASSEMBLY SEQUENCE

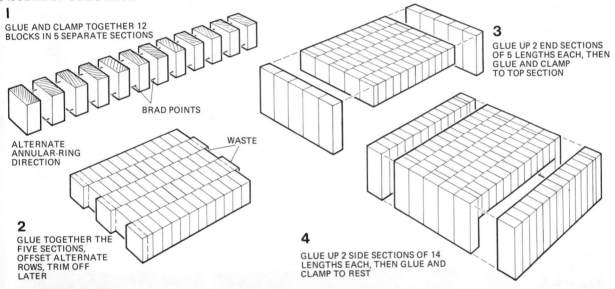

1 GLUE AND CLAMP TOGETHER 12 BLOCKS IN 5 SEPARATE SECTIONS

BRAD POINTS

ALTERNATE ANNULAR-RING DIRECTION

WASTE

2 GLUE TOGETHER THE FIVE SECTIONS, OFFSET ALTERNATE ROWS, TRIM OFF LATER

3 GLUE UP 2 END SECTIONS OF 5 LENGTHS EACH, THEN GLUE AND CLAMP TO TOP SECTION

4 GLUE UP 2 SIDE SECTIONS OF 14 LENGTHS EACH, THEN GLUE AND CLAMP TO REST

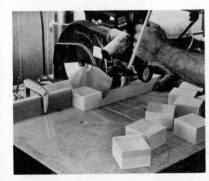

STOP BLOCK clamped to saw's fence, plus smooth-cutting blade, gives uniform blocks with nonsplintered edges.

ALTERNATE annular rings of blocks, number blocks and insert headless brads in one side to prevent shifting when gluing.

SAW TABLE and rip fence, plus board, make alignment setup for imbedding brads with bar clamp. No glue is used here.

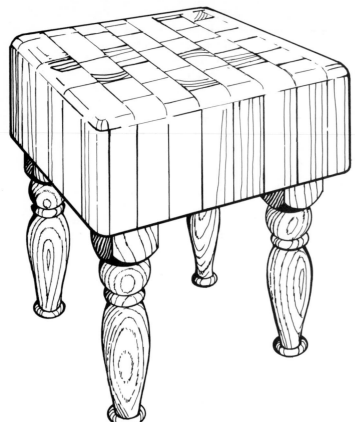

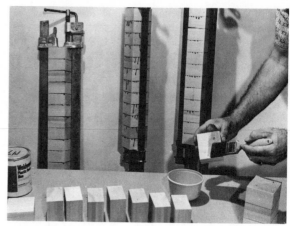

WORK FAST when gluing. Coat both surfaces thoroughly, stack blocks vertically, and use two bar clamps on each stack.

LINE UP five glued-up stacks so joints are offset, then mark the projections for cutting off the waste at alternate ends.

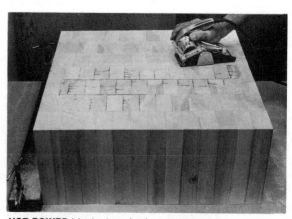

USE POWER block plane for fast surfacing of top, hand plane otherwise. Follow planing with belt and finishing sanders.

Make 60 blocks for the top

You'll find it best to work with easy-to-handle short lengths of about two feet. Rip and joint each piece exactly alike, then make the cross cuts to come up with 60 small blocks 3 in. long. All rip and jointing cuts must be perfectly square.

Gluing the block is done in stages. Five rows of 12 blocks each are made up to start the top. Pairs of headless nails are used in all phases of gluing line-up to insure the necessary accuracy. Use 1-in. No. 17-ga. nails with the heads clipped off. Drill pilot holes in all alternate faces to a depth that will allow about ¼ in. of the points to protrude. Line up a dozen of the short blocks on the saw table and up against the rip fence, then clamp a straight piece of wood onto the table and up against the blocks to keep them in perfect alignment. Apply a bar clamp over the stack, then slowly tighten it to drive the nail points into each mating piece. Number the blocks, then separate them for gluing.

ROUGH-ROUND leg blanks with gouge and run lathe at medium speed. Parting-tool depth cuts simplify turning four duplicate legs.

CLAMP THE LEGS in place for drilling the pilot holes for 3/8x4½-in. lagscrews. Tighten the lagscrews before you remove the holding clamp.

RUN A SERIES of kerf cuts to form a notch at the top of each leg. Hold the work securely against the fence with your hand (not shown in photo for clarity).

APPLY ONE coat of special wood-bowl finish; it produces excellent hard topping. The finish was applied to the legs while each was still in the lathe.

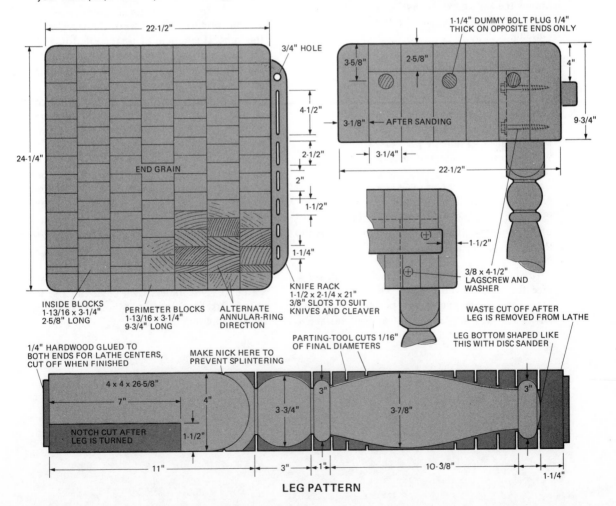

22-1/2"

3/4" HOLE

24-1/4"

END GRAIN

4-1/2"

2-1/2"

2"

1-1/2"

1-1/4"

KNIFE RACK
1-1/2 x 2-1/4 x 21"
3/8" SLOTS TO SUIT
KNIVES AND CLEAVER

INSIDE BLOCKS
1-13/16 x 3-1/4"
2-5/8" LONG

PERIMETER BLOCKS
1-13/16 x 3-1/4"
9-3/4" LONG

ALTERNATE
ANNULAR-RING
DIRECTION

1-1/4" DUMMY BOLT PLUG 1/4"
THICK ON OPPOSITE ENDS ONLY

3-5/8"   2-5/8"   4"

3-1/8" ← AFTER SANDING

9-3/4"

3-1/4"

22-1/2"

1-1/2"

3/8 x 4-1/2"
LAGSCREW AND
WASHER

WASTE CUT OFF AFTER
LEG IS REMOVED FROM LATHE

PARTING-TOOL CUTS 1/16"
OF FINAL DIAMETERS

LEG BOTTOM SHAPED LIKE
THIS WITH DISC SANDER

1/4" HARDWOOD GLUED TO
BOTH ENDS FOR LATHE CENTERS,
CUT OFF WHEN FINISHED

MAKE NICK HERE TO
PREVENT SPLINTERING

4 x 4 x 26-5/8"

7"   4"   3"   3"

3-3/4"   3-7/8"

NOTCH CUT AFTER
LEG IS TURNED   1-1/2"

11"   3"   1"   10-3/8"   1-1/4"

LEG PATTERN

Use water-resistant, plastic resin glue and a postage scale for accurate proportioning of powder and water. This is important: If too thin, a mix will be weak: too heavy, it may begin to set before you get all the pieces together. Work with vertical stacks; brush a coat of glue on both surfaces, then insert the nailpoints into the holes of the stacked pieces. Apply pressure to the stack with two bar clamps. If you wait about an hour before scraping off the excess glue, it will come off much easier and with less mess. When the glue has dried, joint the surfaces of each block slightly to remove all traces of excess glue before proceeding to the next gluing step.

Line up the five stacks so an offset joint pattern results. This will necessitate cutting off a bit of waste on alternate ends. The offset pattern does two things: It makes a stronger top and adds visual interest. Follow the same procedure with a pair of headless nail-positioning pins to align the five stacks for gluing. When the basic top is glued, it will measure approximately 3 x 16 x 20¾ in. Joint the four sides, then put the piece aside while you work on the end blocks. The drawing shows the top thickness as 2⅝ in.; this reflects the removal of stock in the final planing and sanding.

Make up two ends consisting of five 10-in. pieces glued edge to edge and two side pieces composed of 14 lengths glued face to face. Note that one block of half-thickness is required in each of the two side assemblies. Use temporary clamped-on cleats during the gluing to insure that the surfaces glue up perfectly true. Kitchen wax paper will prevent the cleats from sticking to the work.

Dummy bolt plugs are used for effect on the end blocks. Drill shallow holes, about ¼ in. deep by 1½ in. in diameter, then plug them with slices of thick dowel of the same size which you turn on the lathe. Position them so the grain runs clockwise.

If you have a power block plane, you can surface the top with little effort. Otherwise you'll need a jack plane and muscle power. Round off all corners with a plane, then sand all surfaces with a belt sander followed with a finishing sander. Apply a coat of sealer only to the inside surfaces to protect the wood against dampness. A special nontoxic salad bowl sealer is available. Apply one coat of the salad-bowl seal using a full brush and letting it soak in.

Glue up blocks for the legs

The lathe work is next. Glue up the stock for the turning blocks and joint them to 4 in. square. Glue a scrap of extra-hard wood, such as maple or oak, to each end to provide durable temporary centers which will not readily wear during the rough turning. Use the gouge to rough-round the cylindrical section, but first make a shallow nick cut at the shoulder using the heel of the skew held vertically. This will prevent accidental splintering of square corners. After rounding carefully, make parting cuts to the required depths as indicated on the drawing. Shape contours with skew and diamond-point chisels, working to limits set by parting-tool grooves. Sand smooth.

To obtain a top-rate finish, apply several coats of your preferred finish while the work is still in the lathe. If you plan to use the salad-bowl finish for the entire job, it will take a full pint. When the finish coats are dry, saw off the waste. If you sand a slight convex curve on the bottoms of the legs, you'll be able to get by without casters, which would somewhat spoil the appearance. Shallow rounded ends will permit easy sliding on practically any floor.

Most dado cutters haven't the capacity to make the deep cuts required for notching the legs so a series of kerf cuts is made to clear out waste. You can use a table saw or radial saw, but the latter is preferred since repeated pushing of the leg on a table saw may mar the finish. The legs are secured with a pair of ⅜ x 4½-in. hex-head lagscrews. Glue is optional.

Finally the knife rack. Make it by boring a series of ⅜-in. holes, then clear out the waste with a chisel to form slots. Glue the rack in place before applying the finish.

Butcher block furniture

■ YOU CAN BRING butcher block out of the kitchen and show off its beautiful wood grain in your living room with this sofa, chair and coffee table. They're designed for rapid construction, rugged use and contemporary style.

The same methods are used to build a chair and sofa. We'll detail the chair, and if you make the sofa, just substitute the dimensions on the

exploded drawing.

Cut a 2-in. thick, 30 x 72-in. butcher block slab into two 35⅞ x 29⅞-in. pieces. Orient the sides to hide or minimize blemishes. For shadow skids (a visual detail that makes the furniture "float"), rip 2 in. off the bottom of each side and trim skids to dimensions shown to give a ¼-in. reveal around the edges that meet the butcher block sides.

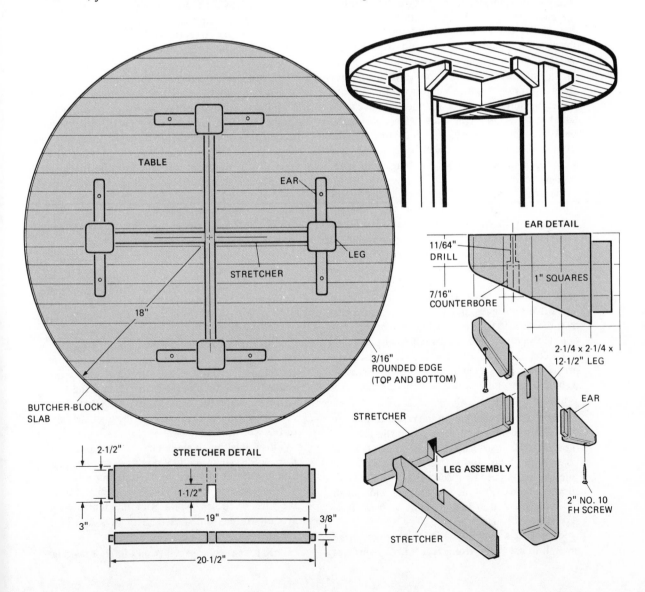

For the fascias, rip two 32½-in. lengths 6¼-in. wide from 4/4 maple. Sand down all butcher block and 4/4 maple pieces, finishing with No. 220 grit. Then, with a ³/₁₆-in. self-guided rounding-over bit, kill all the hard edges except along the base of the large side panels.

Stain the skids ebony for contrast and, when they're dry, apply teak oil to the surfaces. Attach the skids to the side pieces with ⁵/₁₆ x 3-in. lagbolts and washers only, with ⅞-in. dia. counterbores for wrench clearance.

Poplar framing and cleats

● Base framing: Cut all base members and cleats from 5/4 poplar and assemble with glue and 2-in. No. 10 FH screws. Drop the cleats ⅝ in. down from the top edge of the base frame.
● Back frame: Rip enough 5/4 poplar to frame the back and fasten the ends with glue and 2-in. No. 10 FH screws. Finish by adding the two ⅜-in. plywood panels with glue and 4d box nails.
● Upholstery: Seating dimensions are a key part of a comfortable couch. If you're pretty tall (or short), you might want to adjust the proportions of the furniture. The back and the seat have to be soft but firm. One-inch foam is enough on the back, but the seat cushions need more flexible support. On this plan, the seat is supported by a weave of 2-in.-wide rubber webbing, with ¾-in. spacing between rows.

Start each strip by nailing one edge to the cleat with two No. 14 tacks. Then fold the webbing over, hiding the first two tacks, and drive home two more tacks through the doubled webbing.

With one end tacked and the other end stretched across the frame, put a 2½-lb. weight at the half-way point. Adjust the webbing tension until the weight forces the webbing ½ in. down and drive two tacks into the second cleat. Fold over the flap, drive in two more tacks through the doubled webbing and cut away the surplus.

To complete the seat, use the same fastening procedure on the remaining sides and weave the webbing over and under, alternating rows as you go.

Install 1-in.-thick foam in the recess formed by the sides and rails and edge-staple the foam to the cleats. Then stretch No. 40, heavy-duty muslin over the foam and staple it to the rails and sides at the edges. You don't need single, large sheets of foam to do the job. Smaller widths can be butt-jointed into larger sheets with contact-type rubber cement.

Start with a piece of 1-in.-thick foam large enough to cover the front, rear and top surfaces of the back, and spray these surfaces with contact cement. Spray the entire inside surface of the foam and, when dry, roll the foam smoothly around the three surfaces of the back. You can trim the edges flush with a utility knife.

This layer should also be covered with muslin and stapled on the sides and bottom where it won't show.

Stretching fabric

To keep fabric wrinkle-free as you stretch it over a surface, drive a tack (or staple) at the midpoint of one edge. Then stretch the material toward the corners, drive a fastener at each end and tack down the space in between. Repeat this procedure on the remaining three sides, removing any scalloping as you go along with additional fasteners. If your fabric has a nap (smooth when stroked in one direction and rough in the other), place it so the smooth stroke goes toward the *front* on the base and *down* the front face of the back.

If you use a patterned fabric, you'll have to check the pattern alignment from back to base.

Fabric usually comes in 45 or 54-in.-wide bolts. This will have no effect on the chair, but center seams will be required for the sofa.

Align the fabric on the base, stretch it out, and fasten it to the front rail face and the blocking piece with staples or tacks. Stretch the fabric crosswise and drive all fasteners into the side faces where they won't be seen.

On the back, make sure that fasteners are driven into the bottom and sides. Some tucking or slitting may be necessary at the top outside edges of the back.

For now, leave a 6-in.-long "tail" of fabric at the lower rear edge of the back.

Assembling the pieces

Attach the back to the base with ⁵/₁₆ x 2½-in. lagbolts and washers. They are screwed in from the bottom surface of the blocking piece—the space between the intermediate (C) and the rear (B) rails. Align the back so that the fabric-covered foam protrudes about ¾ in. beyond the face of the rear rail in the base.

This is the time to make sure the base and back form a 90° angle. If they don't, loosen the lags and add shims to make up the difference.

Now stretch the "tail" down and fasten it to the face of the rear rail. Run the fabric ends around corners and fasten them at sides. This completes your back-base assembly.

Drill four evenly spaced ⁵/₁₆-in.-dia. holes along

THE COMFORTABLE seat is supported by rubber webbing. Use a tack hammer to drive the No. 14 tacks.

WEBBING is recessed into frame to provide room for 1-in. foam. Staple to cleats and cover with muslin.

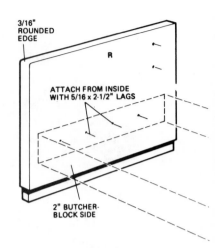

3/16" ROUNDED EDGE

R

ATTACH FROM INSIDE WITH 5/16 x 2-1/2" LAGS

2" BUTCHER-BLOCK SIDE

BUTCHER-BLOCK COUCH

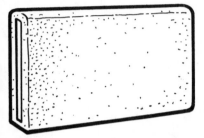

FOAM IS applied to back frame with contact cement; then edges are turned and stapled at bottom and sides.

AFTER ATTACHING back to base, staple 6-in. "tail" of fabric from the back onto the rear seat rail.

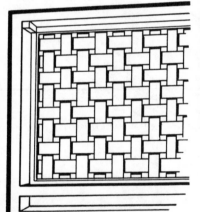

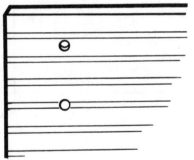

LAGBOLTING IS DONE through the space between the two back rails (top). In the side panels, legs are recessed and covered with maple plugs. To keep the fabric wrinkle-free, make "hospital" corners all around. Electric stapler is timesaver.

the horizontal centerline of the poplar base sides and punch-mark the inside of the butcher block sides through these holes for alignment.Using a ¼-in. bit, drill the punch marks 1½-in. deep to accept the lagbolts.

From the outside of the butcher-block side panels, drill and counterbore the two holes to install the ⁵⁄₁₆ x 2½-in. lags and washers.

Complete the chair by trimming the ends of the fascias to the exact length between the butcher block sides. Fasten them to the rails from the inside with 1½-in. No. 10 FH screws.

Making the table

You can make coffee-table legs out of almost anything from clay flue tile to cast-iron pipe. If you stick to maple, rip enough 4/4 maple to laminate four legs (three pieces in each) 2¼ x 12½ in. long. Machine a ⅜ x 2¼ x ¾-in. mortise on three sides of the legs, starting ⅜ in. from the top.

Rip two stretchers and eight "ears" from 4/4 maple (check dimensions shown). Machine the tenons on ends of the "ears" and notch each stretcher at its midpoint to lock the assembly.

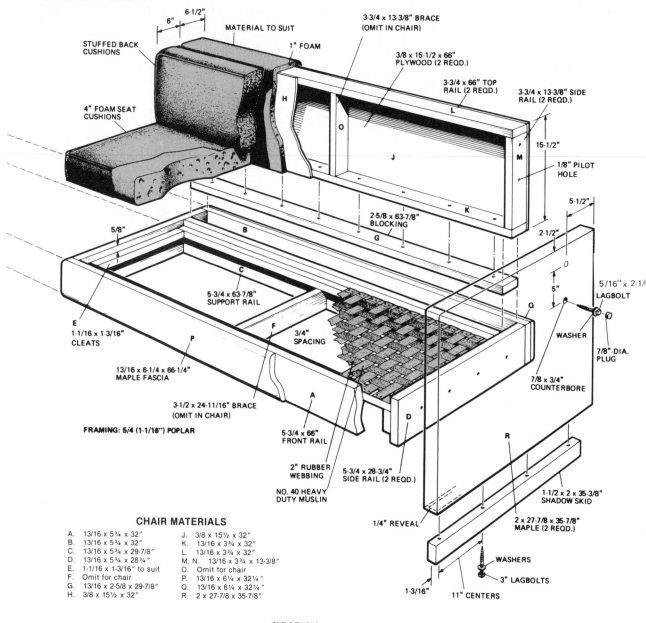

6" 6-1/2"

MATERIAL TO SUIT

STUFFED BACK CUSHIONS

1" FOAM

3-3/4 x 13-3/8" BRACE (OMIT IN CHAIR)

3/8 x 15-1/2 x 66" PLYWOOD (2 REQD.)

3-3/4 x 66" TOP RAIL (2 REQD.)

3-3/4 x 13-3/8" SIDE RAIL (2 REQD.)

4" FOAM SEAT CUSHIONS

H

O

L

J

M

15-1/2"

1/8" PILOT HOLE

K

2-5/8 x 63-7/8" BLOCKING

G

5-1/2"

2-1/2"

5/8"

B

O

C

5"

Q

5/16" x 2-1/ LAGBOLT

5-3/4 x 63-7/8" SUPPORT RAIL

E

F

3/4" SPACING

WASHER

7/8"-DIA. PLUG

1-1/16 x 1-3/16" CLEATS

P

7/8 x 3/4" COUNTERBORE

13/16 x 6-1/4 x 66-1/4" MAPLE FASCIA

A

D

R

3-1/2 x 24-11/16" BRACE (OMIT IN CHAIR)

5-3/4 x 66" FRONT RAIL

FRAMING: 5/4 (1-1/16") POPLAR

2" RUBBER WEBBING

5-3/4 x 28-3/4" SIDE RAIL (2 REQD.)

NO. 40 HEAVY DUTY MUSLIN

1-1/2 x 2 x 35-3/8" SHADOW SKID

2 x 27-7/8 x 35-7/8" MAPLE (2 REQD.)

1/4" REVEAL

WASHERS

3" LAGBOLTS

1-3/16"

11" CENTERS

CHAIR MATERIALS

A. 13/16 x 5¾ x 32"
B. 13/16 x 5¾ x 32"
C. 13/16 x 5¾ x 29-7/8"
D. 13/16 x 5¾ x 28¾"
E. 1-1/16 x 1-3/16" to suit
F. Omit for chair
G. 13/16 x 2-5/8 x 29-7/8"
H. 3/8 x 15½ x 32"

J. 3/8 x 15½ x 32"
K. 13/16 x 3¾ x 32"
L. 13/16 x 3¾ x 32"
M, N. 13/16 x 3¾ x 13-3/8"
O. Omit for chair
P. 13/16 x 6¼ x 32¼"
Q. 13/16 x 6¼ x 32¼"
R. 2 x 27-7/8 x 35-7/8"

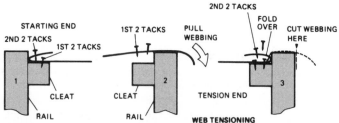

STARTING END

2ND 2 TACKS
1ST 2 TACKS

1

CLEAT

RAIL

1ST 2 TACKS

2

CLEAT

RAIL

PULL WEBBING

2ND 2 TACKS

FOLD OVER

CUT WEBBING HERE

3

TENSION END

WEB TENSIONING

Clamp and glue these pieces as a single unit on a flat surface to assure complete contact with the bottom of the 36-in.-dia. tabletop.

To complete the table, place the top (good surface down) on a rug with the leg assembly centered. Drill and counterbore each "ear" for 2-in.

No. 10 FH screws. Mark the tabletop through these holes, drill the pilots and assemble.

For a really pleasing finish, rub oiled surfaces (when dry) with 000 steel wool. Apply another thin coat of oil, rub wet surfaces with 0000 wool and remove the excess with a lintfree cloth.

Cabinets: a place for everything

■ AND EVERYTHING in its place. The old adage points up the usefulness of cabinets. Name anything portable and there's probably a cabinet designed for it.

The cabinet in our history

In the households of a century or more ago, cabinets were the only storage places. Every bedroom had its armoire, a cabinet for personal wardrobe, because few homes had bedroom closets. Every dining room and kitchen had its corner cabinet or hutch where dishes, flatware and cooking utensils were stored. Chests and chests of drawers of yesteryear held the linens we store in our modern linen closets.

In those early years, cabinetmakers held highly respected positions in their community. Their knowledge and skill were reflected in the quality of workmanship and determined the price of their products. Tools were simple hand tools, because there were none of the power tools which make today's woodworking so much easier. They worked largely with handsaws, miter boxes, hand chisels, brace and bits, clamps, squares, various planes, shaves, scrapers and sanding blocks. Some may have had a pedal-operated lathe.

Cabinetmakers may also have cut their own lumber from trees near home or shop, air-drying it in a lean-to shed. If so, they had to plane each board to the desired thickness and surface each to an acceptable smoothness. While they had access to wider boards than can be found today, sizable panels were still fabricated by gluing and clamping. This meant board edges had to be hand-planed so they would mate precisely, with no gaps. Without the machines that do the work today, each mortise and tenon was chiseled by hand, each peg hole bored at precise angles, dovetail joints cut with meticulous accuracy. Many even painstakingly fashioned their own hardware. Many of the most treasured antiques are the results of months of cabinetmakers' labor.

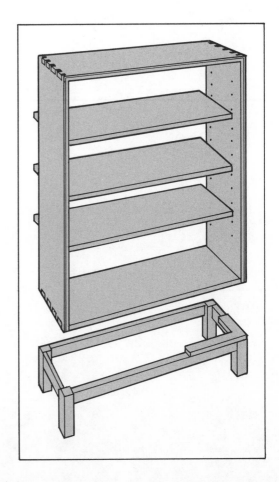

Cabinetmaking today

Today's cabinetmaking hobbyist has several precision power tools available that can reduce months of hand labor to a relatively few hours. They include the table saw, band saw, radial-arm saw, jigsaw, accurate miter saw, power planer, drill press, portable and pin routers, and belt, disc or drum sanders. Many have accessories that expand their usefulness. In addition to these power tools, there are numerous precision hand tools, guides and gauges that speed cabinetmaking and make it more pleasure than work.

There is also pleasure, however, in fashioning things by hand, and those who have been active woodworkers come to appreciate the feel of quality hand tools. Knowing which plane to use for each task, for example, can be as personally satisfying as knowing which club is right for a particular golf shot.

Joinery

Cabinetmaking is largely a matter of joinery. Where corners meet, where legs attach, where rails meet stile, where top joins frame—there

you'll find a joint. The way you make the joint determines its beauty and its strength. All joints should be clamped until the glue thoroughly dries.

Glue supports the joint, but its mechanical structure does the holding. You'll need a large number of bar clamps and C-clamps when building a cabinet to effectively hold the joints and assure a squared-up cabinet. When forming a frame, you can guarantee square corners and a square frame by the 3-4-5 method: Measure 3 ft. along one side; 4 ft. along the other. The distance between these two points completing a triangle should be 5 ft. if the corner is square. It may be necessary sometimes to put a long pipe clamp corner to corner to bring a rectangle corner to square.

Joint types

There is a substantial number of different joint types. Each has its own character and usefulness.

Butt joint. A glued or butt joint is used when two or more boards are joined over their length, as when a solid wood panel is desired. Sometimes rabbet, tongue-and-groove, splines, or dowel pins are also used to strengthen the joint. When planing boards for a butt joint, give the centers a slight hollow. When glued and clamped, this will ensure a snug, even fit along the whole length of

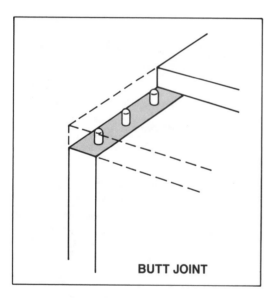

BUTT JOINT

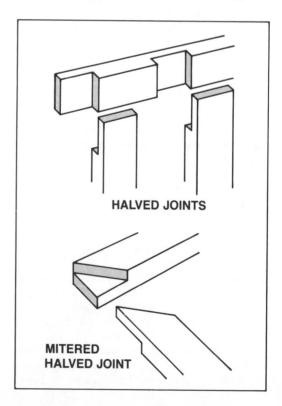

HALVED JOINTS

MITERED HALVED JOINT

the joint. Variations on the butt joint are the *coopered joint,* which uses the same flat butt mating but at an angle. It is used when several boards are mated to form a curved shape, as you might want for a window planter.

Halved joint. A halved joint is possibly the simplest for joining at right angles. It requires the addition of a screw or nail to secure it. As its name indicates, half of one component is mated with half of another so the original thickness of each is maintained at the joint. A variation on this joint is a mitered halving, in which each half is mitered to join the other.

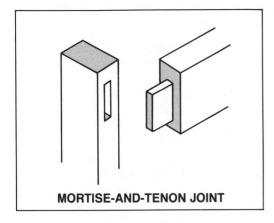

MORTISE-AND-TENON JOINT

Mortise-and-tenon. Mortise-and-tenon joints are strong and will hold tight, especially when glued. Used where rail meets stile, a mortise is cut at center point on the stile, and a tenon is cut at the end of the rail and fitted to the width and depth of the mortise. These joints should be dry-fit before glue is applied to ensure a tight, snug mating of the two. The twin-tenon joint uses two tenons mating with two mortises and is used for legs on a heavy piece, such as a large cabinet.

Dovetail joints. Originally, dovetail joints were confined to elements of a cabinet that would not show, such as back corners of drawers. The dovetail, however, is attractive in its own way, and more and more woodworkers are displaying the dovetail prominently as a decorative element. The dovetail is aptly named: A series of shapes like the tail of a dove are cut into one component and are mated with another series cut so they interlock. Some dovetail joints expose both end grains. Others have the component mortised to accept the dovetails and so conceal the end grain and display only one face of the dovetail.

Doweled mitered joints. Mitered joints are another simplified joint form. They require dowel pins to hold securely. A doweled joint is bored to accept one or more dowel pins and glued. Holes are bored only deep enough to accept half the down pin's length and are not visible when the joint is closed. Doweled joints are frequently used when legs join the frame or where rails meet stiles.

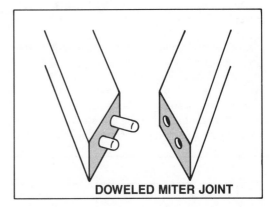

DOWELED MITER JOINT

Keyed mitered joints. Keyed miters are sometimes used for corners that are to be covered by veneer. After the mitered joint is made and glue has dried, the corner is sawn several times to accept tight-fitting veneer keys. The keys are glued in and cut off level with the surfaces of the corner.

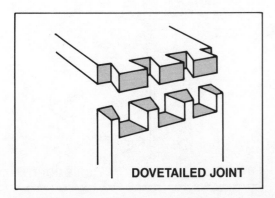

DOVETAILED JOINT

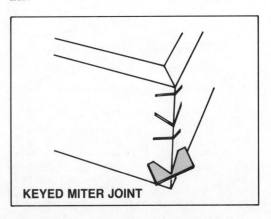

KEYED MITER JOINT

Housed joint. A housed joint is generally used where shelving is part of a cabinet. In this case, the thickness of the shelf board fits into a kerf routed into the sides. A simple housed joint will have a kerf cut to fit the entire width of the shelf. A stopped housed joint conceals the kerf at the front.

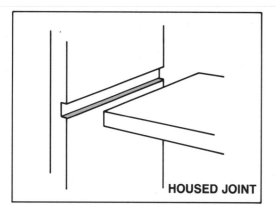

HOUSED JOINT

Tongue-and-groove joint. A tongue-and-groove joint is just what it implies: A tongue cut in one piece is fitted to a groove cut in the other. This joint is frequently used when creating panels with a planked appearance. It is also used when making a floating panel in which the several boards forming the panel are dry-butted and contained in a frame.

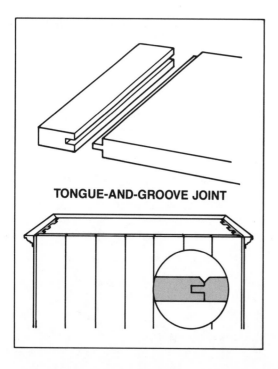

TONGUE-AND-GROOVE JOINT

Lapped joint. In a lapped joint, one component is rabbeted to accept the other. Sometimes, both are rabbeted to mate, concealing the end grain of one.

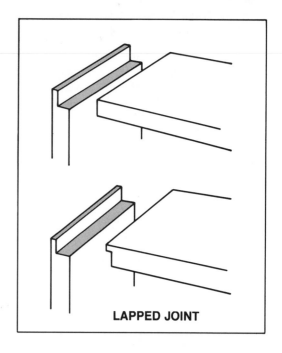

LAPPED JOINT

Rule joint. Sometimes a cabinet requires a joint that is free to move—the leaf of a drop-leaf table is typical. Hinged on the underside, the tabletop has a routed edge. The leaf swings up to conceal the routed edge of the tabletop and give the appearance of a flat surface. This is called a rule joint. Other moving joints are a finger joint and knuckle joint.

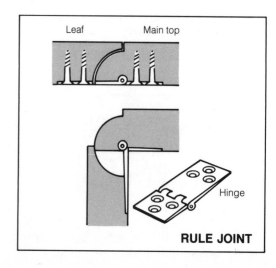

Leaf   Main top

Hinge

RULE JOINT

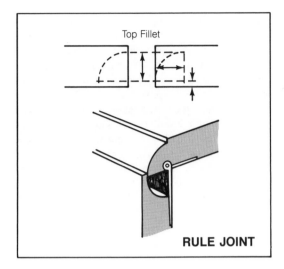

RULE JOINT

Joining sheet material

Today's woodworker has materials our turn-of-the-century predecessors could not imagine. Plywood and particleboard save hours of tedious labor required to produce large panels from individual boards. These materials can be veneered with hardwoods that would make the turn-of-the-century cabinetmaker envious. But, like the materials the early cabinetmaker used, plywood and particle wood have to be joined.

Tongue-and-groove joints for plywood. There is a joint when the edge of the veneered plywood is faced with a molding trim. Usually these are tongue-and-groove joints. Frequently the tongue is cut in the molding and the groove in the edge of the plywood. Sometimes, a loose tongue is fitted with grooves to cut in both pieces.

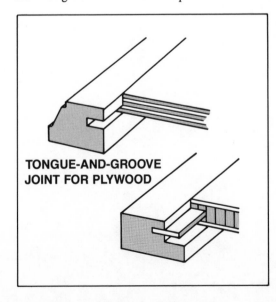

TONGUE-AND-GROOVE JOINT FOR PLYWOOD

Dovetail joints for plywood. Dovetail joints can be effectively used when joining two plywood panels. As with solid wood, dovetails can be partially concealed.

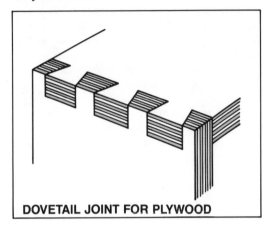

DOVETAIL JOINT FOR PLYWOOD

Mortise-and-tenon joints for plywood. You can use the mortise-and-tenon concept for joining plywood panels at a corner. A series of tenons is cut along the length of one panel. These are fitted into mortises cut into the other.

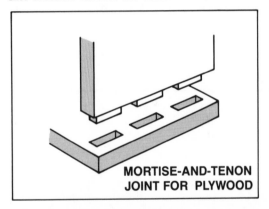

MORTISE-AND-TENON JOINT FOR PLYWOOD

Corner block joints for plywood. Corner blocks constitute another method for joining plywood panels. Corner blocks are glued into the inside corner of the joint and are screwed in place to tightly secure the corner.

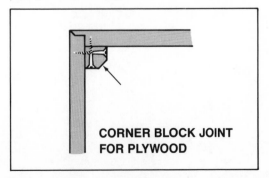

CORNER BLOCK JOINT FOR PLYWOOD

Do-it-yourself cabinet projects

On the following pages you'll find help with just about any cabinet project you want to undertake.

Cabinets to make a room illustrates shop-built cabinets for your living or dining room with doors that feature strips of wood arranged in chevron fashion.

Multipurpose wall cabinets provide a clean, modern design of built-in cabinets to satisfy a host of storage and entertainment needs and are designed with both form and function in mind.

A Colonial pie safe gives you help in duplicating this piece of American country furniture with pierced tin panels on the doors, used in the 1700s to hold pies, bread, and sometimes meat.

The Colonial cupboard for your china is a charming, colorful Early American reproduction, and its glass doors offers the perfect setting to display your best china.

How to install kitchen cabinets gives a series of hints, tips and architectural standards to meet just about any challenge in putting new cabinets in your kitchen.

Space adders for crowded kitchens gives four handy places to add that needed storage in your kitchen—places you may never have thought of for solving some of your storage needs.

Cabinets to make a room

■ TO MAKE THIS living room multifunctional, one end was elevated and the walls banked with custom-designed cabinets and drawers. Now the space serves as a dining room and study. It provides the effect of a separate room, yet has a spacious feeling that's not constrained by a dividing partition.

Planning and materials

Your first step should be to decide on the number of cabinets the room requires, and then figure out what materials you'll need to buy. These three cabinets shown were built to fit along one wall. To make three cabinets, you need two 4 × 8-ft. sheets of ¾-in. birch plywood for the tops, bottoms and sides. Use ⅛-in. birch plywood for the back.

Making the cabinets

Cut the ¾-in. sheets into three equal strips 15⅞ in. × 8 ft. Cut the tops and bottoms (A), and the sides (B). Use a table saw or router to cut rabbets on the tops and bottoms. Cut dadoes in the sides. Be sure to wear eye protection.

A ¼-in. groove at the back inside edge of each piece receives the plywood back (C). Join all pieces with carpenter's glue. Cut and install the shelf cleats (D,E) and the shelf (F) with its edging (G).

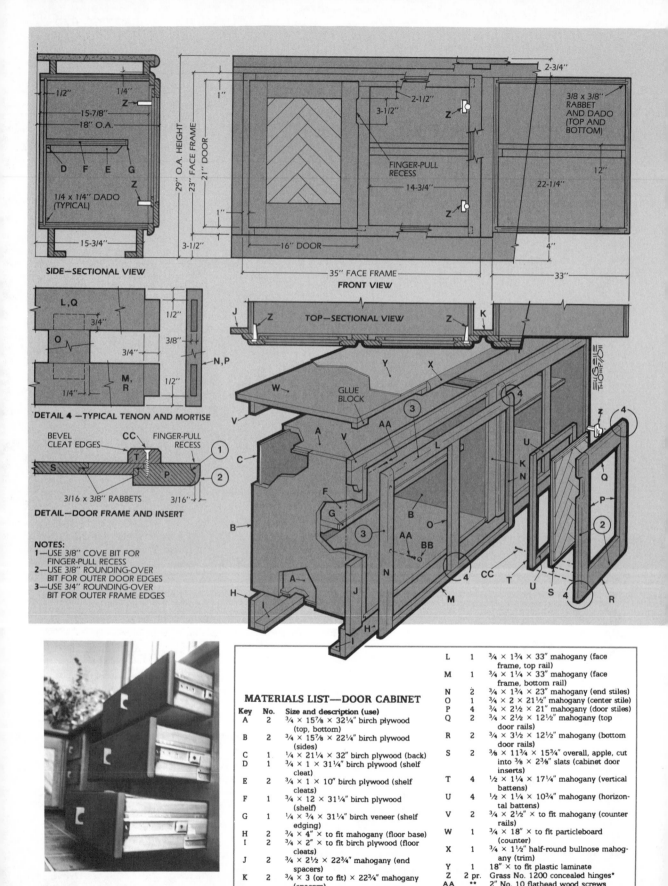

SIDE—SECTIONAL VIEW

1/2″
1/4″
Z
15-7/8″
18″ O.A.
D F E G
1/4 x 1/4″ DADO (TYPICAL)
Z
15-3/4″

29″ O.A. HEIGHT
23″ FACE FRAME
21″ DOOR
1″
1″
3-1/2″

2-1/2″
3-1/2″
Z
FINGER-PULL RECESS
14-3/4″
Z

2-3/4″
3/8 x 3/8″ RABBET AND DADO (TOP AND BOTTOM)
12″
22-1/4″
4″

16″ DOOR
35″ FACE FRAME
33″
FRONT VIEW

TOP—SECTIONAL VIEW
J Z
Z K

L,Q
1/2″
O
3/4″
3/8″
3/4″
N,P
M,R
1/4″
1/2″

DETAIL 4 —TYPICAL TENON AND MORTISE

BEVEL CLEAT EDGES
CC
FINGER-PULL RECESS
T
S
P
1
2
3/16 x 3/8″ RABBETS
3/16″

DETAIL—DOOR FRAME AND INSERT

NOTES:
1—USE 3/8″ COVE BIT FOR FINGER-PULL RECESS
2—USE 3/8″ ROUNDING-OVER BIT FOR OUTER DOOR EDGES
3—USE 3/4″ ROUNDING-OVER BIT FOR OUTER FRAME EDGES

Y X
W
GLUE BLOCK
V
A V AA 3
C
L
U
Z 4
F
K N
Q
G
4
B
O
P
3
AA BB
N
CC T U S R
H J M 2
I

MATERIALS LIST—DOOR CABINET

Key	No.	Size and description (use)
A	2	¾ × 15⅞ × 32¼″ birch plywood (top, bottom)
B	2	¾ × 15⅞ × 22¼″ birch plywood (sides)
C	1	¼ × 21¼ × 32″ birch plywood (back)
D	1	¾ × 1 × 31¼″ birch plywood (shelf cleat)
E	2	¾ × 1 × 10″ birch plywood (shelf cleats)
F	1	¾ × 12 × 31¼″ birch plywood (shelf)
G	1	¼ × ¾ × 31¼″ birch veneer (shelf edging)
H	2	¾ × 4″ × to fit mahogany (floor base)
I	2	¾ × 2″ × to fit birch plywood (floor cleats)
J	2	¾ × 2½ × 22¾″ mahogany (end spacers)
K	2	¾ × 3 (or to fit) × 22¾″ mahogany (spacers)
L	1	¾ × 1¾ × 33″ mahogany (face frame, top rail)
M	1	¾ × 1¼ × 33″ mahogany (face frame, bottom rail)
N	2	¾ × 1¾ × 23″ mahogany (end stiles)
O	1	¾ × 2 × 21½″ mahogany (center stile)
P	4	¾ × 2½ × 21″ mahogany (door stiles)
Q	2	¾ × 2½ × 12½″ mahogany (top door rails)
R	2	¾ × 3½ × 12½″ mahogany (bottom door rails)
S	2	⅜ × 11¾ × 15¾″ overall, apple, cut into ⅜ × 2⅜″ slats (cabinet door inserts)
T	4	½ × 1¼ × 17¼″ mahogany (vertical battens)
U	4	½ × 1¼ × 10¾″ mahogany (horizontal battens)
V	2	¾ × 2½″ × to fit mahogany (counter rails)
W	1	¾ × 18″ × to fit particleboard (counter)
X	1	¾ × 1½″ half-round bullnose mahogany (trim)
Y	1	18″ × to fit plastic laminate
Z	2 pr.	Grass No. 1200 concealed hinges*
AA	**	2″ No. 10 flathead wood screws
BB	**	Wood plugs
CC	**	1″ No. 8 flathead wood screws

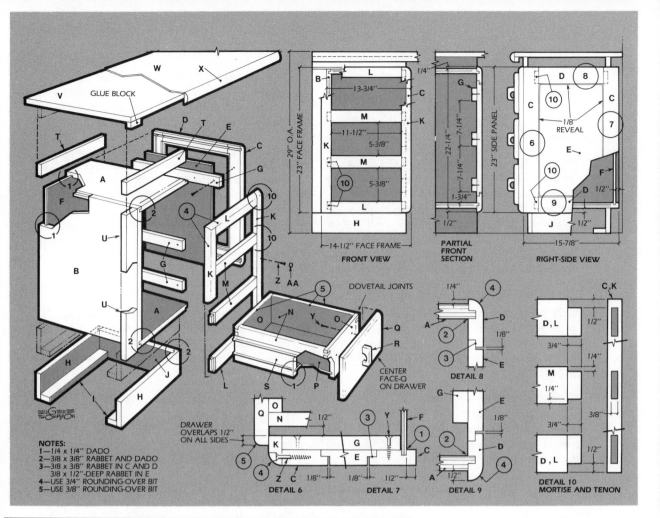

NOTES:
1—1/4 x 1/4" DADO
2—3/8 x 3/8" RABBET AND DADO
3—3/8 x 3/8" RABBET IN C AND D
3/8 x 1/2"-DEEP RABBET IN E
4—USE 3/4" ROUNDING-OVER BIT
5—USE 3/8" ROUNDING-OVER BIT

MATERIALS LIST—DRAWER CABINET

Key	No.	Size and description (use)
A	2	$3/4 \times 15^{7}/8 \times 13$" birch plywood (top, bottom)
B	1	$3/4 \times 15^{7}/8 \times 22^{1}/4$" birch plywood (side)
C	2	$3/4 \times 2^{1}/2 \times 23$" mahogany (side stiles)
D	2	$3/4 \times 2^{1}/2 \times 12^{3}/8$" mahogany (side rails)
E	1	$3/4 \times 11^{5}/8 \times 18^{3}/4$" mahogany (side insert)
F	1	$1/4 \times 12^{3}/4 \times 21^{1}/4$" birch plywood (back)
G	3	$3/4 \times 2 \times 15$" birch plywood (cleats to fasten insert and mount drawer guides)
H	2	$3/4 \times 4 \times 15^{1}/4$" mahogany (floor base)
I	2	$3/4 \times 2 \times 14^{1}/2$" birch plywood (floor cleats)
J	1	$3/4 \times 4 \times 13$" mahogany (floor base end)
K	2	$3/4 \times 1^{1}/2 \times 23$" mahogany (face frame stiles)
L	2	$3/4 \times 1^{1}/2 \times 13$" mahogany (face frame rails)
M	2	$3/4 \times 1^{15}/16 \times 13$" mahogany (intermediate rails)
N	6	$3/4 \times 5^{1}/8 \times 15$" pine (drawer sides)
O	6	$3/4 \times 5^{1}/8 \times 10^{1}/2$" pine (drawer front/back)
P	3	$1/4 \times 9^{1}/2 \times 14$" birch plywood (drawer bottom)
Q	3	$3/4 \times 6^{3}/8 \times 12^{1}/2$" mahogany (drawer face)
R	3	$1/2 \times 1 \times 2$" mahogany (drawer pulls)
S	3 pr.	14" full extension drawer slides, Grant No. 527
T	2	$3/4 \times 2$" × to fit mahogany (counter rails)
U	1	$3/4 \times 2^{1}/4 \times 22^{3}/4$" mahogany (side spacer)
V	1	$3/4 \times 18$" × to fit particleboard (counter)
W	1	18" × to fit plastic laminate
X	1	$3/4 \times 1^{1}/2$" half-round bullnose mahogany
Y	*	$1^{1}/4$ × No. 8 flathead screws (secure G, O, Q)
Z	*	2" × No. 10 flathead screws (secure K, L, U)
AA	*	Wood plugs for face frame

* As required.

The face framework for each cabinet is of mahogany. Cut the frame parts (L,M,N,O) to size. Members form a mortise-and-tenon joint (see the detail in the drawing). To cut tenons in L, M and O, measure the ¾-in. length of the tenon and mark its shoulder around each piece. Carefully lay out and mark the ⅜-in. tenon thickness. Mark the width of the tenon. Then make the cuts with a radial-arm saw or a table saw with a miter gauge.

Lay out and mark mortises in parts L, M and N. You can remove waste by boring the mortise on a drill press. Clean the mortise with a sharp chisel or use a hollow chisel attachment on a drill press. Glue and clamp together the face frame. After the glue has set, secure the face frame to the cabinet with counterbored screws (AA), covering them with dowel plugs (BB). Sand the plugs flush. Use a ¾-in. rounding-over bit to break the front edges of the face frame.

The door frames (P,Q,R) are mortised and tenoned together the same way as the face frames. After joining the door frames, rabbet their inside back edges with a router and a ⅜-in. rabbet bit to receive the decorative panel (S, see door frame and insert detail).

Cut the 3½-in.-long recessed finger pull in the door stile 2½-in. from the top. First, use a ⅜-in. cove bit to rout the pull area on the back of the frame. Then use a ⅜-in. rounding-over bit along the outside edges of the frame front, except in the pull area. To cut the edge opposite the pull, place the router at each end of the cove cut and make a light pencil mark at the base apex. Make two more marks 3/16 in. from these marks. Clamp a straightedge on these marks for the shoe to ride against as you cut the pull area, or do the rounding-over step first.

Constructing the door inserts

The inserts (panels) for these cabinets are made of wood from a half-dead apple tree. Delicate lines and tones are created in the dying wood by the process of decay. You may opt for inserts of more readily available material.

Harvesting the wood must be done at the right time. If left too long, the wood will be too decayed to use. If taken too soon, the special seasoned effect is minimal. First, the logs are sliced with a chain saw. After they've been planed and resawn into 3/8. x 2-in. slats, the beauty of the slightly decayed wood shines. You can visually weight the panels by placing the darker strips at the bottom and the lighter ones above. The slats are rabbeted and lap-jointed. Joint the slat edges and finish-sand with 220-grit paper before gluing them together with carpenter's glue.

Cover each glued insert panel with a sheet of waxed paper and ¾-in. plywood and leave them overnight. Next, trim the insert square and rabbet the edges. Then sand the new corners and slightly round the edges. After finishing the doors (as described later), position the inserts in the frames. Secure them with battens (T,U). Do not glue the inserts in place or they'll buckle and break.

Finishing the cabinets

The finishing method here is fast and easy. You can get spectacular results the first time. First, sand the wood with successively finer grits of paper, beginning with 80-grit and ending with

220. Next, flood the surface with penetrating oil. After the oil has penetrated, leaving a light film on the surface, use a high-speed orbital sander with a felt pad base and 400-grit wet or dry silicon carbide paper. Sand the wet surface, adding fresh oil as needed to keep the surface wet.

The high rpm on the sander ensures a silky-smooth finish. Use this method in a well-ventilated room, and take precautions for working with a flammable material.

After sanding and finishing, put the cabinets in place on a base and cleats (H,I). Cut spacers (fillers J,K) of mahogany and fasten them in place with screws through the cabinet stiles. The fillers should be flush with the face frame at the top and extend slightly beyond the toekick below.

Install the doors using concealed hinges (Z). Lay out and cut the door stile as needed for the door-hinge piece. Locate and screw the hinge plate to the cabinet side wall. Adjust the doors as needed by loosening and tightening the adjustment screws.

You can then add the top rails (V) to the entire assembly and install the countertop (W), according to the directions given later. If you are building cabinets with drawers, however, begin work on these, and add the countertop when all units are in position.

Making the drawers

The cabinets with drawers are constructed the same way as the cabinets with doors. The interior sides that are visible (see right-side view in drawing) are made up of rails (D) and stiles (C), with decorative inserts (E) fastened by cleats (G). These sides define a kneehole area so the counter can be used as a desk.

The drawers are assembled with dovetailed corners. You can make them using a template and a ½-in. dovetail cutter in a router. Rout the groove for the bottom piece (P) in the sides and back of the drawer. Round over the edges of the drawer with a ⅜-in. rounding-over bit. Note: Do not round over the false-front edges that abut the drawer front.

Cut the drawer fronts (Q) and drawer pulls (R). Round over the front edges with a ⅜-in. rounding-over bit. Glue and screw the front to the drawer (false front). Apply finish to the cabinet and the drawers as previously described. Then attach the drawers with full-extension slides (S) or other hardware. Install spacers (U) as needed and put the cabinets in place on the base (toekick). Install the counter rails (T) to receive the counter.

THREE CABINETS with face frames rest on the floor toekick along one wall in the room. The vertical mahogany fillers are installed between each of the cabinet units.

DOOR FRAME is smoothed by 400-grit wet/dry silicon carbide paper on orbital sander. Penetrating oil finish is next.

AFTER WOOD slats are glued up, insert dimensions are marked and panel is cut out. Next: Rabbet the edges.

A VIEW of door back shows finger pull, battens holding door panel and concealed hinge on the door stile.

Making the countertop

Cut out the countertop and laminate it. The countertop shown is covered with solid beige plastic laminate. Be sure to cut the laminate about ¼ in. larger than the countertop's length and width. Trim it later, after it's bonded.

The 1½-in. bullnose molding was bought at a lumberyard. But you can make your own molding using 13/16 x 1½-in. mahogany and a ¾-in. rounding-over bit in a router. Glue the molding on and reinforce the joint with glue blocks below.

When you install the countertop, it helps to have an assistant. If you must make the counter in two parts, you can pull the joint together with joint fasteners.

Multipurpose wall cabinets

■ THESE CABINETS were designed with both form and function in mind. They give a clean, contemporary appearance *and* plenty of room to accommodate a generous sampling of today's popular home entertainment equipment.

Included are two tape decks, a stereo receiver and speakers, a turntable on a sliding shelf, a television, and a slide projector on a pullout section of the countertop that allows for convenient image projection on an adjacent wall. All this—and there is still room left over for storing records, tapes, books and other items.

THESE CABINETS can accommodate a wide variety of entertainment equipment, including a slide projector on a center pull-out shelf.

Construction steps

Begin by making the base for the lower cabinets. Cut the plywood and the supports to size, then screw the front plywood rail to the face of the front support. Next, screw the plywood base to the top of the front support as shown in the drawing. If your base is over 8 ft. long, the platform must be built from two pieces of plywood, spliced in the middle.

Cover the base top and front with plastic laminate, using contact cement. Carefully follow the directions on the container of the cement you use.

Next, attach the rear base support to the room wall by driving 3½-in. No. 10 flathead screws through the support and into the wall studs. Make sure this support is installed level.

Place the finished base over the rear support and attach it with screws driven down through the base and into the support. Position these screws so they'll be covered by the cabinets later.

Building in a shadow line

Cut all base cabinet sides, bottoms, tops and backs to size. Be sure to cut the ½ x 1-in.-deep notch at the bottom front corner of all the sides. This "recess," and the ½-in.-wide space between the three middle cabinets and the countertop, are design features. They give a shadow line between all the units that makes the cabinets appear to float.

Apply laminate to the inside surfaces of all the cabinet parts and to the front edges exposed to view. Assemble with countersunk 1¼-in. No. 10

flathead screws driven through the sides into the edges of the tops and bottoms. Be sure each cabinet is square before installing the back. Determine the number and position of the shelves you want. Then, cut the shelves to size and apply laminate to the top and front edge of each. Install with countersunk screws through the sides and into the shelf edges.

Once the shelves are installed, cover the outside cabinet surfaces with laminate as indicated on the drawing.

The cabinets bordering the open speaker areas should have laminate over the entire exposed side. On the cabinets joined directly to each other, all that's required is a 2-in. strip on the sides to cover the plywood that's visible in front of the recessed spacer cleats. A 2-in.-wide strip is also applied to the cabinet tops, except on the center cabinet. It should be covered entirely with laminate so when the slide projector shelf is pulled out, the plywood will not be seen.

Build the drawer cabinets and drawers as shown, then install the drawers, using full extension slides. These cabinets were designed so the drawer side edges would be set in ⅜ in. from the perimeter of the cabinet *and* with a ⅜-in. space between each drawer front. It's not necessary to cover the inside surfaces of the drawer cabinets with laminate.

Determine the best position for your cabinets along the platform base—or use the positions indicated—and install the cleats (parts D and E on the drawing). These cleats keep the individual cabinets from shifting side to side without the need for actually joining them to the base.

Cut a panel from ¼-in.-thick plywood to back

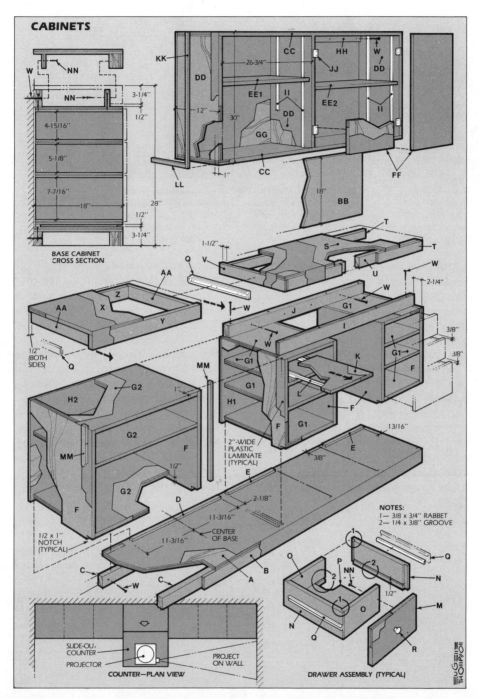

up the open speaker areas, and cover it with laminate. Make it slightly wider than the opening so that when the cabinets are attached to the wall it will be held in place. If you want to avoid the expense of making these panels, simply paint the rear wall with a color to match the laminate.

Place the lower cabinets on the base, starting with the end cabinets. Then position the middle cabinet. Cut the spacers (part M) to size, cover their front edges with laminate and screw to the side of the middle cabinet as shown. Place the last two cabinets on the base.

Install the countertop cleats (parts J and I) across the cabinet tops. Then attach the rear cleat to the wall, making sure to hit at least two studs per cleat. Build and laminate the stationary countertops as shown. Be sure to cover the ends of these tops with laminate, too, so that when the

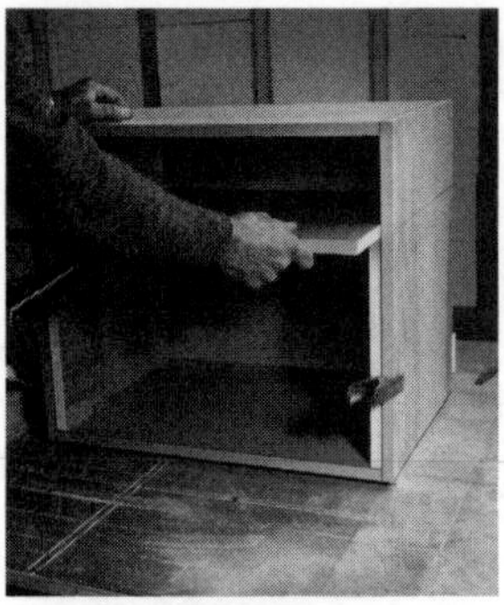

ASSEMBLE CABINET "box," then cut shelf and cover with laminate. Position shelf with scrap blocks clamped as shown.

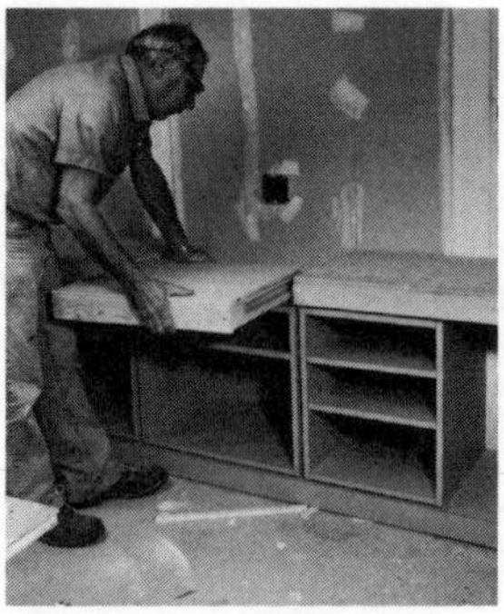

ASSEMBLE COUNTERTOP parts and position on cabinets to check for fit and operation of sliding shelf. Do not attach.

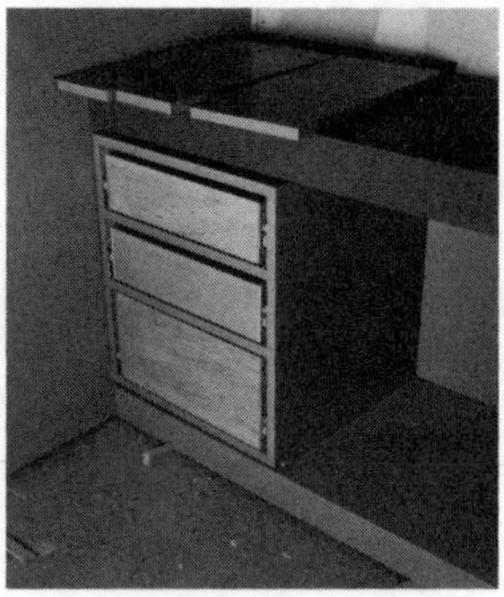

ASSEMBLE DRAWER parts and install with drawer slides. Cover drawer front with laminate, then attach with screws.

slide projector section is pulled out, all the edges will be finished. Install the counters by screwing the rear rail (part T) to the rear cleat (part J). Do this in the open speaker area where both boards are accessible from underneath.

Take the measurement between these two tops to determine the actual size needed for the slide-out top. You should plan on having two 1/16-in.-wide gaps between the three tops *after* the laminate is installed. Build the sliding top and install it with full extension slides hung on the sliding top and the ends of both fixed tops.

Adding the upper cabinets

When the upper cabinets are complete, install one, using the hanging cleat (part HH). Be sure to hit at least two studs in the length of the cleat. Position the other cabinet on the countertop or brace it in position and at the proper height, and measure the distance between the cabinets.

Cut the spacer cleats (parts KK and LL) to match this dimension, cover the front edge with laminate, then remove the second cabinet and attach the strips to the installed cabinet. This method will give you a tight, professional fit.

Install the second upper cabinet and hang all the cabinet doors. Instead of using door pulls, rout out a 3/8-in.-deep by 3-in.-long section of the bottom back door edge to use as a finger grip.

To finish the job, just paint the wall behind the cabinets and countertop, or install panels of burlap-cover fiberboard as illustrated.

MATERIALS LIST
MULTIPURPOSE WALL CABINETS

Key	No.	Size and description (use)
A	1	¾ x 18 x 121″ plywood (base)
B	1	¾ x 2½ x 121″ fir (rail)
C	2	1½ x 2½ x 121″ fir (supports)
D	1	½ x ¾ x 22⅜″ fir (cleat)
E	4	½ x ¾ x 14⅜″ fir (cleats)
F	10	¾ x 17¾ x 21″ plywood (cabinet sides)
G1	15	¾ x 14½ x 17¾″ plywood (small cabinet top, bottom, shelf)
G2	3	¾ x 17¾ x 22½″ plywood (large cabinet top, bottom, shelf)
H1	4	¼ x 16 x 21″ plywood (small cabinet back)
H2	1	¼ x 21 x 24″ plywood (large cabinet back)
I	2	¾ x 3 x 47¼″ fir (cleats)
J	2	¾ x 3 x 47¼″ fir (cleats)
K	1	½ x 14¼ x 16″ plywood (turntable base)
L	1 pr.	14½″ Grant Model A Record Player Slide
M1	4	¾ x 5⅜ x 15⅛″ plywood (small drawer front)
M2	2	¾ x 7⅞ x 15⅛″ plywood (large drawer front)
N1	8	¾ x 4½ x 17½″ plywood (small drawer sides)
N2	4	¾ x 7 x 17½″ plywood (large drawer sides)
O1	8	¾ x 4½ x 12¾″ plywood (small drawer false front, back)
O2	4	¾ x 7 x 12¾″ plywood (large drawer false front, back)
P	6	¼ x 12¾ x 16¾″ plywood (bottom)
Q	7 pr.	16″ Grant No. 328 drawer slide
R	6	Stanley No. 4482 drawer pull
S	2	¾ x 18 x 48½″ plywood (countertop)
T	4	¾ x 2½ x 47¾″ plywood (front, rear rails)
U	2	1½ x 2½ x 47¾″ fir (cleats)
V	2	¾ x 2½ x 18″ plywood (end rails)
W	*	3½″ No. 10 flathead screws
X	1	¾ x 18 x 23⅝″ plywood (countertop)
Y	1	¾ x 2½ x 23⅝″ fir (front rail)
Z	1	¾ x 2½ x 21¼″ fir (back rail)
AA	2	¾ x 2½ x 17¼″ fir (side rails)
BB	1	18 x 121″ burlap-covered fiberboard
CC	4	¾ x 11¾ x 60¼″ plywood (cabinet top, bottom)
DD	6	¾ x 11¾ x 28½″ plywood (cabinet end, divider)
EE1	3	¾ x 11½ x 26¼″ plywood (open cabinet shelf)
EE2	2	¾ x 11½ x 30¾″ plywood (closed cabinet shelf)
FF	4	¾ x 15¾ x 29¼″ plywood (doors)
GG	2	¼ x 30 x 60¼″ plywood (back)
HH	2	¾ x 1½ x 31¼ fir (cleats)
II	16	28½″ shelf standards, with 32 support clips
JJ	4 pr.	Hinge-A-Matic No. 591-26 self-closing overlay door hinges
KK	1	½ x ¾ x 30″ fir (spacer)
LL	1	½ x ¾ x 10¼″ fir (spacer)
MM	2	½ x ¾ x 21½″ fir (spacer)
NN	*	1¼″ No. 10 flathead screws

(*) As required.

Colonial pie safe

■ THE PIE SAFE, variously called the pie cupboard, kitchen safe, tin safe, and even the meat safe, came into use in the 1700s and was made until about 1880. A large cabinet, made to hold pies, bread, and sometimes meat, it had pierced tin panels in the doors and usually on the ends. The tin panels were for ventilation and to keep out insects, but they also served a decorative purpose. Usually, the cabinets had one or two draw-

COLONIAL PIE SAFES no longer cool pies made by the dozen. Modern methods let you bake one pie at a time, so you can use this reproduction of a pie safe as a kitchen cupboard.

ers, most often above, but sometimes below, the tin-paneled doors. The wood was often pine or poplar.

Pie safes are classified as American country furniture and are popular today, particularly among young people. You can buy everything needed to build a reproduction of this popular item at a cost of less than half the prices you'll find at antique shops and auctions. Use No. 2 white pine for the cabinet because it is easy to work, attractive when finished, and materials can be found in nearly any lumberyard. No. 2 white pine is much less costly than clear pine, and a few small knots enhance the appearance of authenticity. By planning saw cuts in advance, you can avoid using stock with large knots or other blemishes.

Start constructing the pie safe by making the doors and side panels. Cut frames from 1-in. stock (actually measuring ¾-in.) Note that door stile K is ¼ in. wider than the other door stiles because the right door overlaps the left. The short horizontal side frame pieces are 4, 5, and 10 in. wide. All other frame parts are 2 in. wide. You can save time by ripping, planing the edges, and sanding all framing stock before assembly.

Cut pieces to the proper length and prepare the joints for mortise and tenons. Cut the ¼-in. rabbet on the door stiles. Test-assemble frames and mark the edges for the tin-panel slots.

Cutting the tin-panel slots

To make this slot, use a fine-tooth plywood blade on your table or radial-arm saw. Set the saw for a cut just over ½ in. deep.

You are now ready to make the pierced tin panels. You may find a brown protective coating on both sides of the tin when you buy it. This coating can be readily removed with paint thinner (mineral spirits) and No. 00 steel wool. Use the steel wool with lengthwise strokes in the final stages.

With standard 20-in.-width flashing tin available in hardware and building material stores, there is no waste, as 6 linear feet provide material for the 10x14-in. panels, leaving 2 in. for a practice strip.

To pierce the panels, you need a round punch, a tool for slotting, and a suitable backing. See the drawing at the end of this article for the shapes of punches you need. A chunk of hardwood, preferably 12 in. or more in diameter and sanded reasonably smooth on one end, makes an ideal backing.

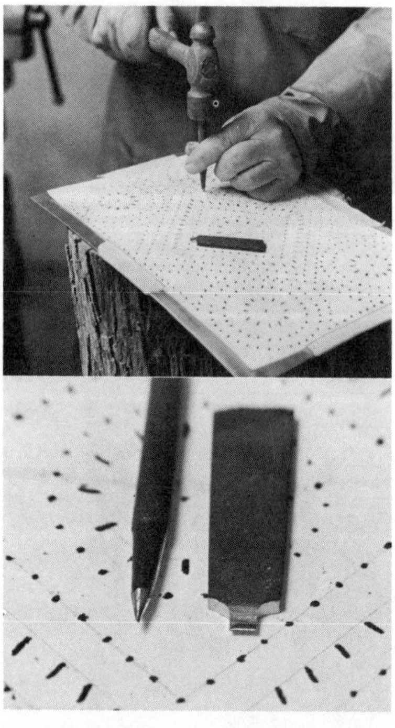

MAKE YOUR piercing tools from a nailset and an 8-in. file. An upright log makes a good work block. The piercing job takes about five hours.

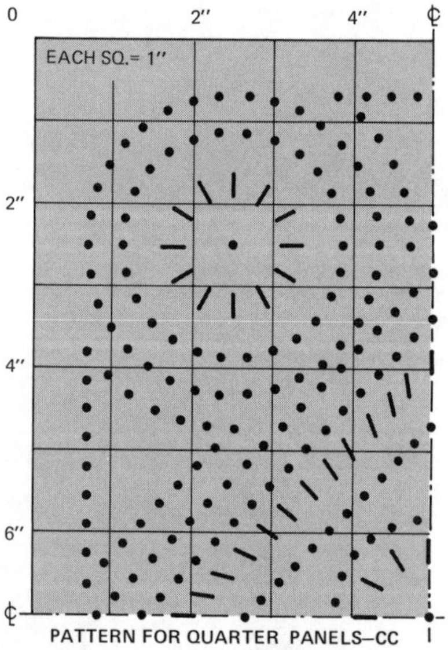
0
2"
4"
℄
EACH SQ.= 1"
2"
4"
6"
℄

PATTERN FOR QUARTER PANELS—CC

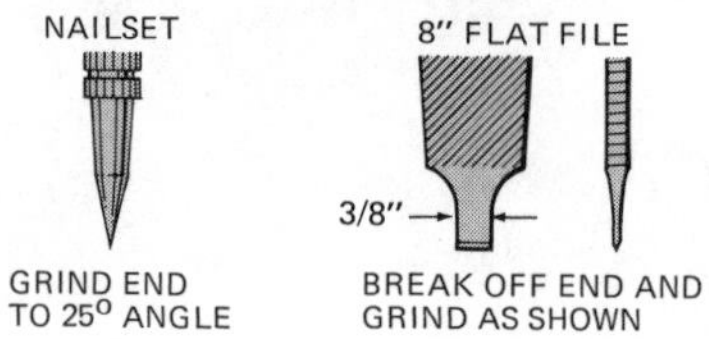
NAILSET
8" FLAT FILE
3/8"
GRIND END
TO 25° ANGLE
BREAK OFF END AND
GRIND AS SHOWN

PIERCING TOOLS

MATERIALS LIST—PIE SAFE

Key	No.	Size and description (use)
A	4	1⅛ × 2 × 55" (frame legs)
B	5	1⅛ × 2 × 35½" (frame rails)
C	2	1⅛ × 2 × 13" (top cleat)
D	1	1⅛ × 2 × 4" (frame stile)
E	1	¾ × 16 × 39½" (top)
F	3	¾ × 13 × 36" (bottom shelf)
G	2	¾ × 10 × 10½" (top side rail)
H	2	¾ × 5 × 10½" (bottom side rail)
I	2	¾ × 4½ × 16½" (drawer front)
J	2	¾ × 4 × 10½" (center side rail)
K	1	¾ × 2¼ × 35" (left door stile)
L	4	¾ × 2 × 47" (side stile)
M	3	¾ × 2 × 35" (door stile)
N	8	¾ × 2 × 14½" (door rails)
O	4	¾ × 1 × 43" (corner cleats)
P	10	¾ × 1 × 13" (cleats)
Q	2	¾ × 1 × 6¾" (runner support)
R	2	¾ × ¾ × 41" (vertical back cleat)
S	2	¾ × ¾ × 32½" (horizontal back cleat)
T	4	¾ × ¾ × 13" (runners)
U	2	¾ × 2 × 4" (corner block)
V	4	½ × 4 × 13½" (drawer side)
W	2	½ × 3½ × 15½" (drawer back)
X	2	½ × 1½ × 13" (inner runner guide)
Y	2	⅜ × 1½ × 13" (outer runner guide)
Z	2	¼ × 34 × 41" (back)
AA	2	¼ × 13¼ × 15½" (drawer bottom)
BB	2	¼ × ¼ × 2" (door stop)
CC	10	10 × 14" No. 28 gauge flashing (tin panel)
DD	3	1½"-dia. wood knob
EE	4	1½" butt hinge
FF	12	2" No. 10 fh screw
GG	*	1¼" No. 10 fh screw
HH	*	¾ No. 10 fh screw
II	*	⅝" No. 5 fh screw
JJ	4	10d finishing nail
KK	*	6d finishing nail
LL	*	1" wire brads

Misc.: Finish, paint thinner, steel wool, carpenter's glue, masking tape. *As required.

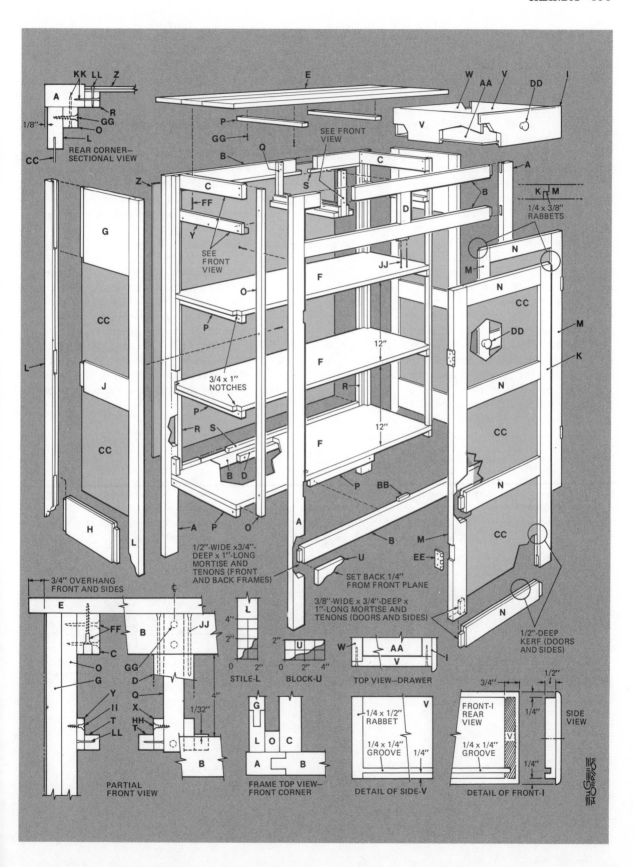

KK LL Z

A
1/8″
R
GG
O
L
CC

REAR CORNER—
SECTIONAL VIEW

E

P
GG

Q

B

Z

SEE FRONT
VIEW

C
FF
Y

SEE
FRONT
VIEW

O

P

3/4 x 1″
NOTCHES

P

R S

B D

A P O

A

G

L

CC

J

CC

H

L

C

S

D

F

JJ

F

12″

F

12″

F

P

BB

B

U

SET BACK 1/4″
FROM FRONT PLANE

3/8″-WIDE x 3/4″-DEEP x
1″-LONG MORTISE AND
TENONS (DOORS AND SIDES)

1/2″-WIDE x3/4″-
DEEP x 1″-LONG
MORTISE AND
TENONS (FRONT
AND BACK FRAMES)

W AA V DD I

V

A

B

K M
1/4 x 3/8″
RABBETS

N

M

N

CC

DD

M

K

N

CC

N

M

EE

CC

N

1/2″-DEEP
KERF (DOORS
AND SIDES)

3/4″ OVERHANG
FRONT AND SIDES

E

FF

B

JJ

C

O

G

GG

D

Y

Q

II

X

T

HH

T

LL

B

PARTIAL
FRONT VIEW

4″

2″

L

0   2″
STILE-L

2″

U

0   2″ 4″
BLOCK-U

G

L O C

A   B

FRAME TOP VIEW—
FRONT CORNER

1/32″

4″

W   AA   I

V

TOP VIEW—DRAWER

1/4 x 1/2″
RABBET

1/4 x 1/4″
GROOVE

V

1/4″

DETAIL OF SIDE-V

3/4″

FRONT-I
REAR
VIEW

1/4 x 1/4″
GROOVE

1/2″

1/4″

V

1/4″

SIDE
VIEW

DETAIL OF FRONT-I

Before you begin piercing the panels, make a few practice holes and slots in a piece of scrap in order to determine the force needed to make the perforations. A lightweight ball-peen hammer does a good job.

The pattern shown was one of the most common in the 19th century. After enlarging the pattern to the 10x14-in. panel size, make two or three extra copies in case you damage one while using it. Secure the pattern to the tin at the corners with masking tape and you are ready to begin the job of piercing.

The panel may tend to curl upward as you work. You can prevent this by tacking it down loosely with a couple of upholstery tacks through perforations already made. Break this job up into several sessions because it can become tedious.

Test-assemble frames again with tin panels before the final assembly with glue. Be sure the panel designs are centered.

Build the front and back frames for the cabinet from 5⁄4 stock (which actually measures about 1⅛ in. thick). Glue the joints and check carefully to be sure the corners remain square when tightening the bar clamps.

Attach the two end panels with flathead wood screws from the inside of the vertical frame cleats. Cut and install the floor of the cabinet by inverting the entire assembly, holding the bottom in place with cleats. Then install the shelves.

Mark the hinge locations on the doors and front frames, mortise, and mount the doors.

Make the runners for the two drawers of maple, cherry, or other close-grained hardwood. Construct the drawers and try them for proper fit before gluing. Turn knobs for the drawers and right door on the lathe or, if you wish, purchase them at a hardware or building supply store.

Make the top of the pie safe by edge-gluing two or more pieces. The plywood back is a piece of plain ¼-in. mahogany wall paneling. Use a piece of the same 4x8-ft. panel for the drawer bottoms.

Now that you have it all together, go around the panel edges with masking tape. Then go over all edges once, not to round them, but to knock off sharpness with No. 180-grit abrasive paper on a sanding block. Dust and tack off.

Select a stain which is appropriate for the wood. After allowing a day for drying, sand lightly with the same grade of paper, clean, apply white shellac to the end grain, and apply polyurethane.

BEGIN construction with doors and sides that contain the tin panels. Test-assemble first for a good fit, then again to center the pattern of each panel.

START construction by attaching the cabinet frame to side panels with ¾-in., No. 10 flathead screws. Screws are countersunk in vertical cleats.

AFTER side panels, doors, shelves and bottom are installed, assemble drawer runners. You will find it easier to work from back and through top.

Colonial cupboard for your china

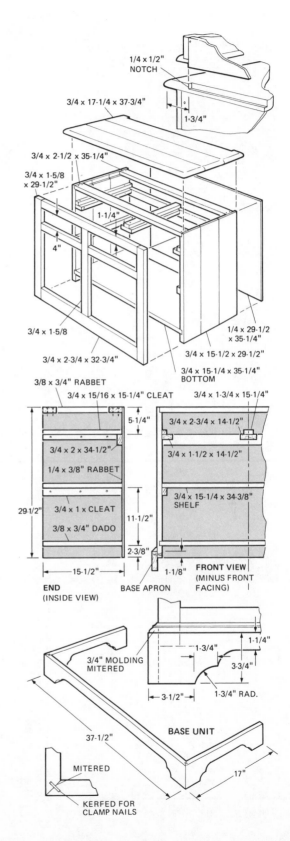

1/4 x 1/2" NOTCH

3/4 x 17-1/4 x 37-3/4"

1-3/4"

3/4 x 2-1/2 x 35-1/4"

3/4 x 1-5/8 x 29-1/2"

1-1/4"

4"

3/4 x 1-5/8

3/4 x 2-3/4 x 32-3/4"

1/4 x 29-1/2 x 35-1/4"

3/4 x 15-1/2 x 29-1/2"

3/4 x 15-1/4 x 35-1/4" BOTTOM

3/8 x 3/4" RABBET

3/4 x 15/16 x 15-1/4" CLEAT

3/4 x 1-3/4 x 15-1/4"

5-1/4"

3/4 x 2-3/4 x 14-1/2"

3/4 x 2 x 34-1/2"

3/4 x 1-1/2 x 14-1/2"

1/4 3/8" RABBET

3/4 x 15-1/4 x 34-3/8" SHELF

29-1/2"

3/4 x 1 x CLEAT

11-1/2"

3/8 x 3/4" DADO

2-3/8"

15-1/2"

1-1/8"

END (INSIDE VIEW)

BASE APRON

FRONT VIEW (MINUS FRONT FACING)

3/4" MOLDING MITERED

1-3/4"

1-1/4"

3-3/4"

3-1/2"

1-3/4" RAD.

BASE UNIT

37-1/2"

17"

MITERED

KERFED FOR CLAMP NAILS

■ CHARMING, COLORFUL and Early American in appearance, this fine version of a Colonial cupboard offers the perfect setting for displaying your best china. It's made of clear pine, a wood that's easy to get at any lumberyard. The piece consists of two basic units, a base and a top, built separately.

The sides of the glass-door cabinet—the upper unit—are recessed into the top of the base unit and the upper unit's back fits into a rabbet in the top of the base. This and a few screws along the back of the top unit weld your Colonial cupboard into a single, reliably rigid combination. Yet, if you decide to move, the whole cupboard breaks down easily into two separate units. You'll find them easily manageable on moving day.

The solid-pine ends and top for the base unit require wide pieces which must be built up of two or more boards. You can join them by simply butt-gluing the edges, but ⅜-in. dowels make the strongest joints. After sanding smooth, cut the ends to the sizes given, then run dadoes on the inside 2⅜ in. up from the bottom and rabbets in the top and rear edges; the rear ones are for a ¼-in. plywood back. You can use fir plywood for the bottom if you wish; it will save gluing-up boards. Use glue alone to hold the bottom in the dadoes and nails plus glue to attach the 2½-in. cross rails in the rabbets at the top. Check the assembly with a square and hold it with a diagonal brace across the front while you cut and add the plywood back.

Round edges of the top along three sides with a portable router or hand plane and run a rabbet in the rear edge as shown to later receive the back panel of the upper unit. Use No. 8 x 1¼-in. flathead screws up through the front and back cross rails to attach the top, but add the top last as this will make it easier to reach in and install the drawer guides.

NAIL DRAWER sides to the fronts in deep end rabbets. Bottoms rest in grooves cut in front and side pieces. Backs fit into side dadoes.

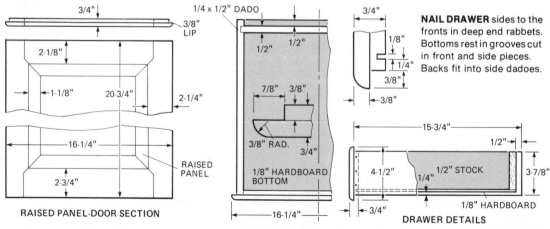

RAISED PANEL-DOOR SECTION

DRAWER DETAILS

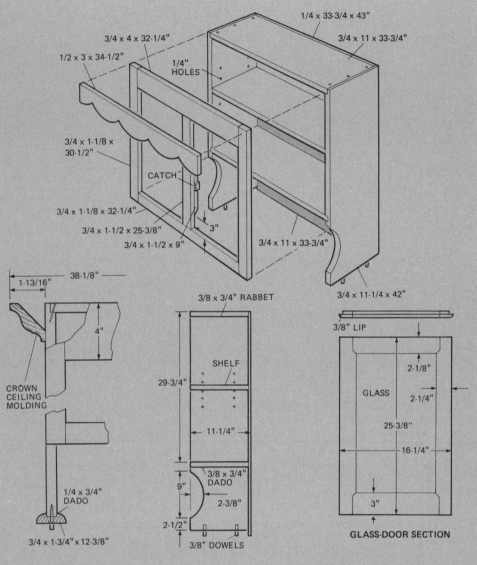

CROWN CEILING MOLDING

GLASS-DOOR SECTION

PARTS LIST

BASE UNIT

No.	Size	Use
2	¾ x 15½ x 29½"	Ends
1	¾ x 15¼ x 35¼"	Bottom
1	¾ x 15¼ x 34⅜"	Shelf
1	¾ x 17¼ x 37¾"	Top
2	¾ x 2½ x 35¼"	Cross members
1	¾ x 2¾ x 32¾"	Front facing (bottom)
2	¾ x 1⅝ x 29½"	Front facing (sides)
2	¾ x 1⅜ x 15⁷/₁₆"	Front facing (center)
1	¾ x 1⅝ x 25½"	Front facing (vertical)
1	¾ x 1¼ x 32¾"	Front facing (top)
2	¾ x 1¼ x 14½"	Drawer guides
2	¾ x ¹⁵/₁₆ x 15¼"	Drawer guides
1	¾ x 1¾ x 15¼"	Drawer guide
1	¾ x 2¾ x 14½"	Drawer guide
2	¾ x 1 x 15¼"	Shelf cleats
1	¾ x 2 x 34½"	Back cleat
2	¾ x 3¾ x 17"	Base apron (sides)
1	¾ x 3¾ x 37½"	Base apron (front)
1	¾ x ¾ x 72"	Base molding
1	¼ x 29½ x 35¼"	Plywood back

UPPER UNIT

No.	Size	Use
2	¾ x 11¼ x 42"	Ends
2	¾ x 11 x 33¾"	Top and bottom
1	¾ x 11 x 33"	Shelf
1	¼ x 33¾ x 43"	Plywood back
1	¾ x 1⅛ x 32¼"	Front facing (bottom)
1	¾ x 1½ x 25⅜"	Front facing (vertical)
2	¾ x 1⅛ x 30½"	Front facing (sides)
1	¾ x 4 x 32¼"	Front facing (top)
1	½ x 3 x 34½"	Scroll facing
1	¾ x 3 x 68"	Crown molding
2	¾ x 1¾ x 12⅜"	End feet
1	¾ x 1½ x 9"	Door-catch cleat

DRAWERS

No.	Size	Use
2	¾ x 4½ x 16¼"	Fronts
4	½ x 3⅞ x 15¾"	Sides
2	½ x 3½ x 15"	Backs
2	⅛ x 15 x 15"	Bottoms

DOORS (BASE)

No.	Size	Use
4	¾ x 2¼ x 20¾"	Side stiles
2	¾ x 2⅛ x 12¾"	Top rails
2	¾ x 2¾ x 12¾"	Bottom rails
2	¾ x 12½ x 16¾"	Raised panels

DOORS (UPPER)

No.	Size	Use
4	¾ x 2¼ x 25"	Side stiles
2	¾ x 3 x 12½"	Bottom rails
2	¾ x 2⅛ x 12½"	Top rails
2	⅛ x 12½ x 20½"	Glass panes
1	¼ x ¼ x 11½"	Quarter-round molding

HARDWARE (BRASS)

No.	Use
4	1"-dia. door knobs
2	3"-wide drawer drop pulls
8	2½" lip-door hinges
4	Spring-loaded, cupboard-door catches

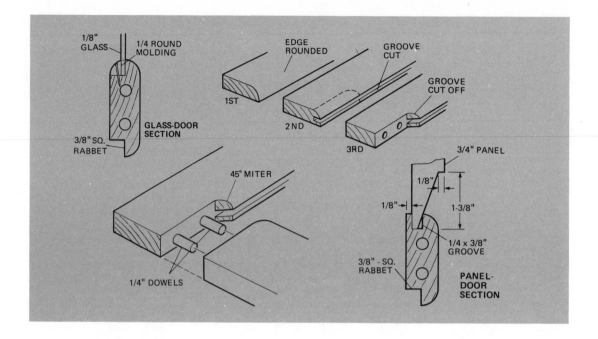

Front edges of the cabinet are covered with a ¾-in.-thick frame. Clamp it together as a separate unit, using dowels and glue to join its seven members. Apply the facing so it is even with the cabinet ends and top cross rail. Use glue, clamps and finishing nails to attach it, then set and putty the heads.

Next, install the drawer guides and shelf cleats following the end and front plan views. Notice that the drawer guides are supported at the back by a 2-in. cross member and placed so they will be in line and even with the drawer openings in the front frame.

The drawers have lip fronts that lap the openings. Use ¾-in. pine for fronts, ½-in. for sides and backs, ⅛-in. hardboard for bottoms. Fronts are rabbeted ⅜ in. top and bottom and ⅞ in. at ends.

The three-piece mitered base laps the front and ends 1⅛ in. Rip it 3¾ in. wide, scroll-cut it and glue and draw the mitered corners together with clamp nails. When dry, attach it from the back with No. 8 x 1¼-in. flathead screws. Finally, miter, glue and brad a molding to finish off the top edges.

The upper unit is simpler to make since the ends, top and bottom are cut from 1x12 boards. Run dadoes and rabbets in the end pieces as before. Sabre-saw the half-moon cutouts and bore a series of ¼-in. holes ¼ in. deep and 1 in.

apart for shelf supports. Rip the top and the bottom 11 in. wide to allow for the ¼-in. back which sits in a rabbet. Before gluing and nailing the two members in place, run plate grooves in the bottom shelf, one 2 in. from the back edge, another 5 in. Make similar grooves in the adjustable middle shelf. Make grooves wide and deep enough to suit your china.

A separate frame, glued and doweled together as before, covers the front edges. Glue it on and use a finishing nail here and there to help hold it. Glue a decorative facing, scroll-cut from ½-in. pine, to the front across the top, then miter crown molding to go around three sides. Finally, glue and screw grooved pieces to lower ends of the uprights.

Put the four door frames together with dowels and rabbet the outer edges so that doors lap the openings. The lower doors are grooved for raised-panel inserts; upper doors are like picture frames, with a rabbet cut all around the inside for window glass. In each case, the grooves and rabbets must be cut before assembly.

The pine-faced plywood back of the upper unit extends ½ in. at the bottom to fit into the rear rabbet in the base unit, and screws are used to hold the two together.

We finished the prototype with a one-coat, brush-on-wipe-off wood finish that gives a patina effect.

Kitchen cabinet installation

■ THERE ARE THREE basic points to keep in mind when you install kitchen cabinets: 1. Base cabinets must be set level, thus shims are usually required. 2. Cabinets must be securely fastened to wall studs. Although many contractors install cabinets using hefty (16d) common nails, proper-size wood screws are a better choice. 3. You must stick to the architectural kitchen standards shown in the drawing at left, below. These dimensions are important; any variance from standard working and reaching heights and depths will result in an uncomfortable-to-work-in kitchen. Also, keep in mind that kitchen cabinets are, in fact, pieces of fine furniture; handle with care to avoid scratching or marring the finish. And keep tools off the countertop.

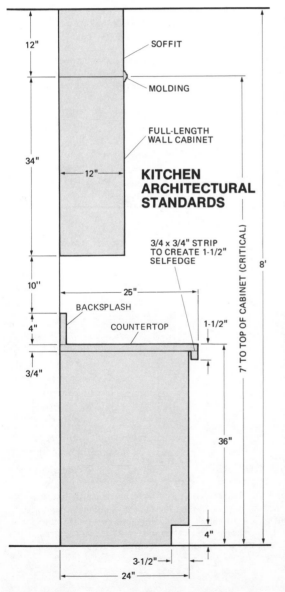

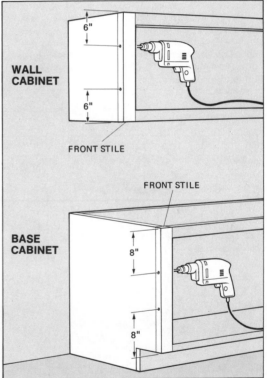

JOINING TWO CABINETS. Start by drilling installation holes in stiles of those cabinets that will butt another. Holes should be large enough for fastening screws to slide freely. Butt the two cabinets and, using each installation hole as a guide, drill a smaller, correct-size pilot hole in the adjacent cabinet's stile. Later, as screws are turned home, they will take their bite in the adjacent stile and pull the joint tightly closed. Hole locations are shown above; for less than full (34 in. high) hangers, usually only one hole is needed at the stile center. Use additional screws wherever the joint is not tight.

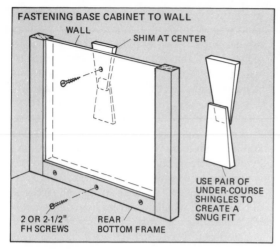

FASTENING BASE CABINET TO WALL

WALL

SHIM AT CENTER

USE PAIR OF UNDER-COURSE SHINGLES TO CREATE A SNUG FIT

2 OR 2-1/2" FH SCREWS

REAR BOTTOM FRAME

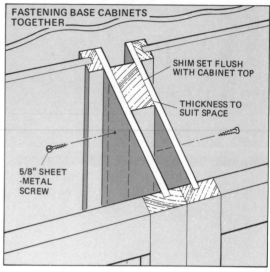

FASTENING BASE CABINETS TOGETHER

SHIM SET FLUSH WITH CABINET TOP

THICKNESS TO SUIT SPACE

5/8" SHEET-METAL SCREW

FASTENING CABINETS TO THE WALL. If it is necessary to drive screws through the back plywood panel to penetrate a wall stud when attaching a base cabinet (above), use shims—undercourse shingles—to assure a rigid installation and to prevent bowing the cabinet's back. Use this method on base cabinets only. For wall cabinets, install 2-in. No. 10 wood screws through the wood fastening rail at the inside top back of the cabinet.

SHIMMING BETWEEN CABINETS. If stiles project beyond sides, use a shim between cabinets as shown. The shim can be of solid wood if the dimension matches stock lumber. For example, if the space between is ¾ in., simply use ¾-in. pine or plywood. For odd dimensions, use a pair of shingles (as shown above, left), to obtain a good snug fit.

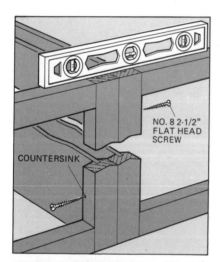

NO. 8 2-1/2" FLAT HEAD SCREW

COUNTERSINK

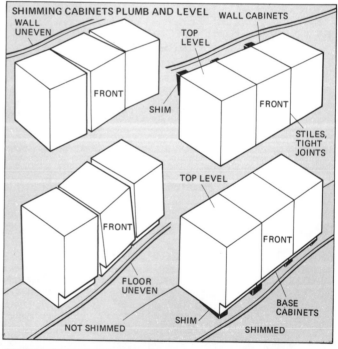

SHIMMING CABINETS PLUMB AND LEVEL

WALL UNEVEN

WALL CABINETS

TOP LEVEL

FRONT

SHIM

FRONT

STILES, TIGHT JOINTS

TOP LEVEL

FRONT

FRONT

FLOOR UNEVEN

NOT SHIMMED

SHIM

BASE CABINETS

SHIMMED

JOINING FRONT FRAMES. Use your spirit level (a 4-footer is best) to level cabinets. Where necessary, slip a shim under a low cabinet to bring it up into the same plane as the fastened first cabinet. When satisfied with alignment and plumb, join the cabinets by installing 2½-in. screws through the installation holes you drilled earlier. Use flathead screws and countersink them so operation of doors, drawers will be smooth.

FLOOR AND WALL SHIMMING. If your floors and walls are not level and plumb, it is a must to shim behind the base and wall cabinets to the highest point as is shown above. Shimming assures proper alignment of horizontal cabinet rails for appearance and is necessary to assure that the doors and drawers will function properly after installation.

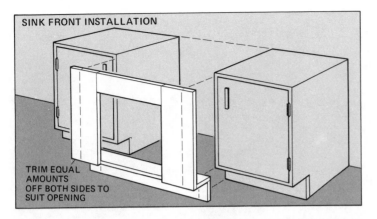

SINK FRONT INSTALLATION

TRIM EQUAL
AMOUNTS
OFF BOTH SIDES TO
SUIT OPENING

SINK-FRONT INSTALLATION.
Generally a sink front (designated SF), not a cabinet, is used below a kitchen sink. Since the most widely used single sink is 24 in. wide and 21 in. deep, most sink fronts come in 24-in. widths. Larger widths for oversize and double sinks are also manufactured. Some makers put extra-wide stiles on the SF so that they can be trimmed to the required size (width) on the job. Sink fronts are secured by fastening through stiles to the side cabinets.

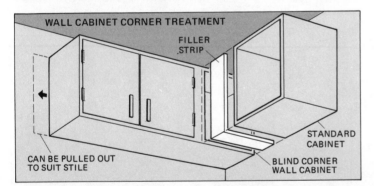

3/4" PLYWOOD
SIDE PANEL

2x2"
CORNER BRACE,
FASTEN TO PANEL
WITH 5/8" SHEET-
METAL SCREWS;
2" SCREWS INTO
WALL AND FLOOR

SINK
FRONT

SPACE FOR
DISHWASHER

DISHWASHER NEXT TO SINK.
If your layout calls for a dishwasher (DW) to be located next to the sink, an extra step will be necessary. Since there is no cabinet for fastening SF on DW side, it is necessary to cut a ¾-in. plywood panel to serve as a sidewall. For rigidity, fasten the plywood "side" to the floor and wall using 2x2-in. corner braces. After countertop is installed, add corner braces from plywood panel to underside of countertop; use ⅝-in. sheet-metal screws to top.

WALL CABINET CORNER TREATMENT

FILLER
STRIP

STANDARD
CABINET

CAN BE PULLED OUT
TO SUIT STILE

BLIND CORNER
WALL CABINET

BLIND CORNER WALL CABINET.
Installation is the same as for other wall-hung cabinets except that a 3-in. filler is used between the blind cabinet and the cabinet butting it at 90° (to assure clearance for door swing). The filler is attached by screws through the hanger cabinet, and from inside the blind corner hanger into the filler. Butting cabinets are hung conventionally using screws through the inside back top rail into the wall studs.

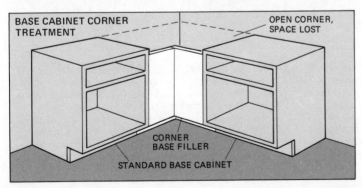

BASE CABINET CORNER
TREATMENT

OPEN CORNER,
SPACE LOST

CORNER
BASE FILLER

STANDARD BASE CABINET

CORNER BASE FILLER.
Base cabinets can be installed as shown at left by using a corner base filler. Though there is a cash saving initially when this type corner is used, it is recommended only for kitchens with ample space. Once closed in, that corner area is space lost for good. To utilize corner space, consider instead installing a blind corner cabinet (BCC).

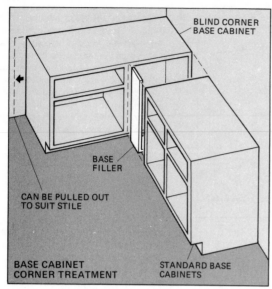

BLIND CORNER
BASE CABINET

BASE
FILLER

CAN BE PULLED OUT
TO SUIT STILE

BASE CABINET
CORNER TREATMENT

STANDARD BASE
CABINETS

BLIND CORNER BASE CABINET. A standard cabinet is installed with filler between it and the blind corner base cabinet (BCC). Fasten the filler with screws through standard cabinet's stile and if possible, with screws through BCC center stile into opposite edge of the filler. Access to corner space is through the standard-cabinet door.

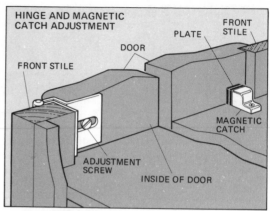

HINGE AND MAGNETIC
CATCH ADJUSTMENT

PLATE

FRONT
STILE

DOOR

FRONT STILE

MAGNETIC
CATCH

ADJUSTMENT
SCREW

INSIDE OF DOOR

ADJUSTING DOORS. Since misalignment of doors and drawers can be caused by rough handling during shipment, most of the manufacturers pack door and drawer adjustment right in with the cabinets. Realignment of these parts generally consists of simply loosening the hinge screws slightly, squaring the doors and retightening the screws. It is also frequently necessary to adjust a magnetic catch; you simply loosen the screws and slide the magnet forward or backward in its slots until the desired contact action has been accomplished. Then retighten the screws.

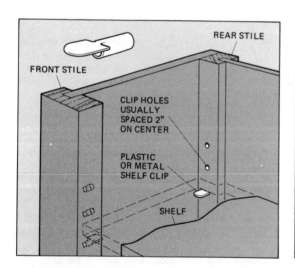

REAR STILE

FRONT STILE

CLIP HOLES
USUALLY
SPACED 2"
ON CENTER

PLASTIC
OR METAL
SHELF CLIP

SHELF

SHELF INSTALLATION. Most base cabinets come with a fixed shelf; full-height wall cabinets usually contain two adjustable shelves. Though there are several kinds of adjustable shelving systems, a commonly used type consists of plastic or metal supports pushed into predrilled holes in wall-cabinet stiles. Simply insert four supports for each shelf and lay it in place. If the shelf rocks, firmly "slap" it in the middle to true up supports and seat the shelf squarely.

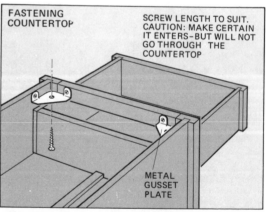

FASTENING
COUNTERTOP

SCREW LENGTH TO SUIT.
CAUTION: MAKE CERTAIN
IT ENTERS–BUT WILL NOT
GO THROUGH THE
COUNTERTOP

METAL
GUSSET
PLATE

INSTALLING THE COUNTERTOP. Usually, base cabinets have metal gusset plates in each corner at the top. These serve a dual purpose: Adding strength to the cabinet and anchoring the countertop. With the countertop in position, carefully measure the length of screw required to obtain a purchase in top's underside without coming through the laminate finish. Not many screws are required here as their primary function is simply to keep the top from shifting laterally.

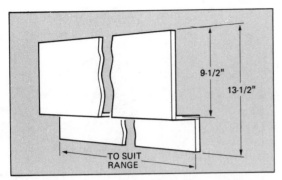

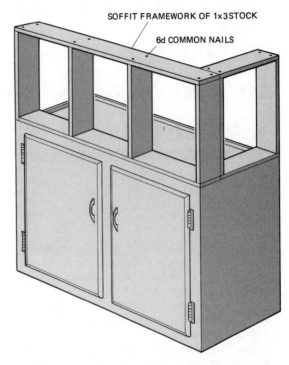

RANGE FRONT FILLER AND PANEL. The range front filler and panel are used when a drop-in range/oven is to be installed. Some ranges call for more elaborate filler pieces than others; thus the range should be picked before the cabinets are ordered and the maker's specifications checked to see if—and what type of—a wood front is needed. A specified size of ¼-in. paneling, finished to match the cabinets, may be all that's required. Bring these specs along when you order the cabinets.

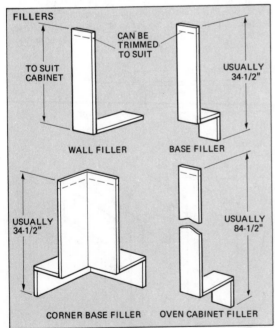

TYPICAL FILLERS. The most commonly used fillers are shown above. Besides serving for blind corner-cabinet installation, these are required when a cabinet run will butt a wall at 90°, and when a wall is so out of plumb or irregular that it will be necessary to scribe (custom-fit) the last cabinet to the wall.

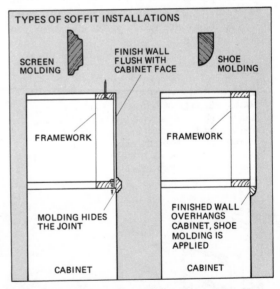

INSTALLING THE SOFFIT. The easiest-to-make soffit enclosure is a ladderlike structure made of 1x3 furring. Take accurate measurements between the cabinet and the ceiling at ends and middle of run and assemble sections on the floor. Then hoist the sections in place and fasten using shims as needed. Framework can be set back a distance equal to thickness of material covering it, or installed flush with the cabinet fronts.

Space adders for crowded kitchens

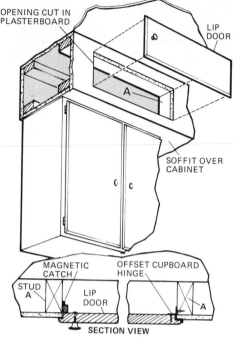

OPENING CUT IN PLASTERBOARD

LIP DOOR

A

SOFFIT OVER CABINET

MAGNETIC CATCH

OFFSET CUPBOARD HINGE

STUD A

LIP DOOR

A

SECTION VIEW

1. Unused Soffit Space

THE DEAD SPACE going to waste within the soffits over kitchen cabinets offers handy storage for items used only on occasion like Christmas dishes and glassware. Make the opening in the plasterboard as large as space permits, then install short studs at the sides to take a lip-type door. Fasten door with a magnetic catch.

STUD

16"

INTERIOR WALL

MAGNETIC CATCH

STUD

SECTION

■ IF YOU'RE HURTING for extra cupboard space and see no way of gaining more, chances are you have overlooked potential storage space that's actually there and going to waste. In some cases it's dead space within a kitchen wall and the soffits over cabinets; in others it's space under wall cabinets and on the surface of a door.

The four space adders shown here show how you can put this waste space to work by building in or adding on shallow cabinets to give extra storage for canned goods, spices and items you don't often use.

2. Piggyback door storage

HANG A SHALLOW cabinet fitted with shelves and a door on the inner surface of a hollow flush door and you'll gain more storage space for can and package goods. Make the cabinet of 1 x 4s, add a dowel railing across each shelf to hold cans in place and hang it with L-brackets and Molly bolts.

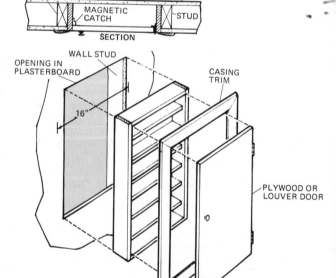

WALL STUD

OPENING IN PLASTERBOARD

16"

CASING TRIM

PLYWOOD OR LOUVER DOOR

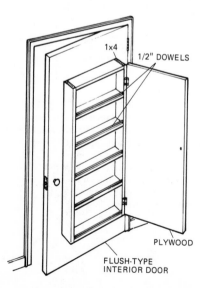

1x4

1/2" DOWELS

PLYWOOD

FLUSH-TYPE INTERIOR DOOR

3. Wall niche for canned goods

HOLLOW SPACE in an interior wall offers storage galore for canned goods. The 3½-in. width of the studs is ample to accept row upon row, one-can deep. The cabinet is made to fit between a pair of studs. The door can be fitted flush with the wall for soup-size (2¼-in.) cans, or it can be brought out an additional ¾ in. by a deeper frame to accept 3-in.-dia. cans. See that the wall is free of pipes and wires.

4. Under-cabinet storage

WITHOUT SACRIFICING counter space, extra storage space can be gained by hanging a row of 4-in. binlike drawers from the underside of your wall cabinets. They're handy for keeping spices, napkins and the like at your fingertips. Each hinged bin pulls out like a drawer and tips down at an angle for full access to contents. The bins ride in a frame assembly attached to the cabinets with screws in counterbored holes. Stop blocks in the grooves prevent the bins from being pulled all the way out.

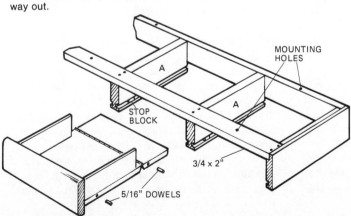

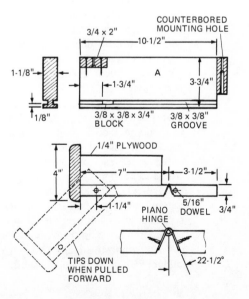

A CENTURY of growth has brought photography from the complex equipment and portable darkrooms of the elite few to the simple devices now common in almost every household.

Cameras—an introduction

■ AFTER MORE THAN a century of constant growth and development, the camera is easing smoothly into the electronic age, incorporating bits and pieces of that modern technology without losing its own identity. This growth shows no signs of slowing down. As a result of this successful blending of the established with the new, we have cameras capable of satisfying the picture-taking needs of a wide variety of users. Today's photographer, from the most casual snapshooter to the most demanding professional, can choose from an almost endless array of models in several formats. Most of these are aided by at least one example of current electronic technology.

Even before the electronic revolution, the photography industry had taken positive steps of its own to ensure its future. The most significant was the incorporation, in the early 1960s, of the exposure meter into the camera body. Combining the camera with one of its most useful accessories not only freed the photographer from the need to carry an extra piece of equipment, it also provided freedom from making decisions. The built-in light measuring device lead to the development of automatic exposure control. Just about every camera now on the market has some form of automation.

Other factors—cheaper production methods, micro chips, inexpensive plastics and the modular concept of design that facilitates repair and replacement—also enabled the camera to assume more and more of the mechanical picture-taking duties. This has given the photographer the freedom to concentrate on either the aesthetic aspect or on nothing at all. Yet with all these advantages, cameras, like most other pieces of machinery, represent a string of compromises. Choosing one that best meets your needs becomes a series of trade-offs.

The disc camera

Curiously enough, a camera's capabilities correspond roughly to the size of its format: the larger the negative, the more versatile and capable the camera. At the simple end of the scale we have the disc camera, a thin, flat box that uses an ultrathin disc containing fifteen 8 × 10mm negatives around the outside edge of the circle. One button controls all the camera's functions, including film advancement and the flash. The flash is built in and fires with each shot (some

THE DISC camera offers point-and-shoot simplicity at the sacrifice of film speed selection and quality enlargements.

disc, this miniature format camera uses small, flat but rectangular and slightly thicker cameras that leave few decisions to the photographer. Film is supplied in a barbell-shaped plastic cartridge with a chamber at each end. Unlike the disc, film advance is manual. Other features, such as focusing or nonfocusing lenses and manual or auto exposure control, vary from model to model. Flash is also automatic, via either a built-in unit or a companion unit that must be attached to the side when needed. Naturally, these models are much smaller and more pocketable when the flash is not attached. Film for 110 cameras comes in 12- or 20-exposure lengths with ISO speeds of 100 or 400. Although there is one black-and-white and one color slide film available (slides must be shown on special 110-size projectors),

only when light levels are low), making this the easiest and quickest of all cameras to operate.

Film choice, however, is limited to one color negative (print) emulsion with an ISO speed rating of 200. Although disc negatives can be enlarged to 5 × 7 in., the standard ("jumbo") 3½ × 5 size is recommended. Some models have built-in meters for auto exposure control, while the more advanced also sport such extras as a self-timer and slide-in close-up or telephoto lens converters.

The 110 camera

Easy film loading is the distinguishing feature of a 110, the next step up the size ladder. Like the

EASY FILM LOADING is the distinguishing feature of the 110 camera, and many models are small enough to fit into a pocket.

TODAY'S CAMERAS appeal to every age and skill level, from the simple point-and-shoot 110 and disc cameras to the electronically sophisticated 35mm and 120 reflex cameras.

110 is aimed primarily at the color print snapshot set. The 13 × 17mm negative generally is enlarged to the standard 3½ × 5-in. size, but under optimum conditions you can get satisfactory 5 × 7 prints.

35mm cameras

By far the most popular and versatile format, 35mm, has benefited most from the technological advancements of the past 50 years. Equally important, all major film breakthroughs have been concentrated in this area. Indeed, the history of photography can be seen in miniature in the history of the 35mm camera. The oldest version of

THE 35MM single-lens reflex cameras offer through-the-lens viewing and focusing systems.

THE CLASSIC 35mm rangefinder camera was once the hallmark of the professional photographer.

the format, the rangefinder type, was once the hallmark of the professional, but now is available from only one manufacturer and is targeted for the serious amateur and pro. In addition to their convenient size and configuration, rangefinder cameras were chiefly noted for their interchangeable lenses—a feature which was, ironically, partially responsible for their downfall.

Single-lens reflex

The successor to the throne is the 35mm single-lens reflex (SLR), largely on the strength of its unique viewing system. By placing a mirror directly behind the lens and a pentaprism viewfinder on top, manufacturers were able to endow this otherwise conventional 35mm camera with a through-the-lens viewing and focusing system. The user gets a properly oriented view of the scene exactly as the film "sees" it. Picture composition, therefore, is extremely easy and accurate. This is a most useful feature, particularly with interchangeable lenses. The SLR's unique ability makes it easier for the photographer to use such

accessories as closeup and copying devices and microscope adapters. The built-in exposure meter is also placed behind the lens so that it, too, can measure what is coming through to the film. The SLR has established itself as the prime tool for all levels of photographers.

Thinking cameras

A decade or so after the first behind-the-lens meter, the integrated circuit micro chip found its

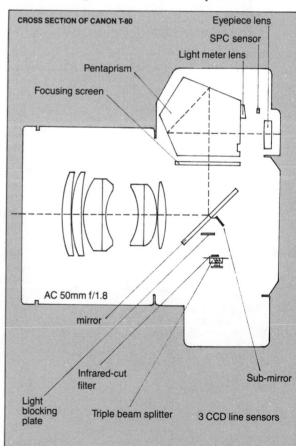

CROSS SECTION OF CANON T-80

Eyepiece lens
SPC sensor
Light meter lens
Pentaprism
Focusing screen
AC 50mm f/1.8
mirror
Infrared-cut filter
Light blocking plate
Triple beam splitter
Sub-mirror
3 CCD line sensors

way into SLR technology. This lead to "thinking" cameras with microcomputers built in. The 35mm SLRs are categorized by their exposure control systems.

Semi-automatic exposure control. The basic SLR resembles the original mechanical models because its exposure control system is semi-automatic, often called match needle or match diode. When taking a meter reading, the user adjusts the lens setting until a needle, or diode, is matched or aligned with an index mark in the viewfinder. It is a system that can be ignored or bypassed in favor of strict manual control. A further advantage to these models is that the battery powers the meter only; all other functions are mechanical. Should the battery fail, the camera will continue to operate but without benefit of a meter.

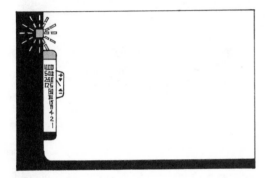

OLDER 35MM SLR cameras allowed exposure control by adjusting lens settings until needle in viewfinder was centered.

Auto exposure. Auto exposure systems fall into three categories. Most common are the aperture-preferred (or priority) and the shutter speed-preferred methods. These require manual setting of either the lens or shutter, with the camera taking care of the other value automatically. For example, on an aperture-preferred camera, you set the lens and the shutter is set by the camera. The third method of automation is the programmed exposure control. This method sets both the lens and the shutter values. Because of the somewhat rigid nature of the programmed system, some manufacturers have developed auto SLRs with multiple programs, individually favoring either a faster shutter speed (for action shots) or a smaller aperture (for greater depth-of-field).

Viewfinder indicators. Many new SLRs provide one, two or all of these auto control systems as well as a manual override. Most have full information viewfinders with some indication of any or all of the following: preferred setting, automatic setting, mode in use, low and high light

TODAY'S CAMERAS have automatic electronic controls for shutter speed, lens opening, focus, flash and film winding.

level warning, flash ready. Although these systems are totally dependent on a working power source (battery), a few provide a single mechanical shutter speed for lost-power emergencies.

Camera systems

Most major SLR cameras are part of a full-fledged system that may include a full range of interchangeable lenses, closeup equipment, motor winders and automatic flash units. There are also special adapters that permit use of the camera with equipment such as microscopes, interchangeable viewfinder prisms and focusing screens. The automatic (dedicated) flash units are geared specifically for use with a particular auto SLR. When properly coupled, the units take over control of the camera's functions, adjusting the amount of flash automatically to achieve a properly exposed picture.

Miniature 35mm

The newest type of 35mm camera is a miniaturized and simplified version of the original range-finder type. Known as compact or point-and-shoot cameras, they feature virtually com-

TODAY'S MINIATURE 35mm cameras feature virtually completely automatic operation of the point-and-shoot cameras but open picture-taking to the wide range of 35mm films available.

plete automatic operation, most notably focusing, at the touch of one button. An infrared or passive triangulation system focuses the lens automatically while the battery power source handles all other functions—exposure control, flash and film advance. These are strictly single fixed-lens models similar to the disc and 110 cameras but with the added advantage of access to the vast number of 35mm films. Some of the simpler models, however, are intended only for color print films so their meters have limited (sometimes just 100 and 400) ISO speed settings.

Roll film cameras

Roll film cameras, those using 120 film (2¼ in.), are intended for more serious photographers who want a larger negative that can be enlarged more successfully. They are either amateur-oriented fixed-lens twin-lens reflex models or professional-quality 120 SLRs which produce pictures in three different formats: straight 2¼ × 2¼ in., 2¼ × 2¾ in or 2¼ × 1⅝ in. These are heavier, bigger and less versatile than their 35mm counterparts.

Future breakthroughs

With the intrusion of electronics, the camera world has become extremely volatile in recent years. Fortunately, each innovation is calculated to make the photographer's life easier. Among the more significant, late-breaking developments are DX-coded film and the growing use of lithium batteries. The DX-coded film in electronically encoded cassettes transmits information (ISO rating, for example) to computer-equipped

THE SINGLE-LENS reflex camera taking the larger 120 film is still the choice of most serious photographers.

cameras with matching DX contacts. Longer-life lithium batteries should go a long way toward solving the battery failure problem bedeviling automatic camera owners and may very well influence design and engineering features on future cameras as well.

How to buy a good used camera

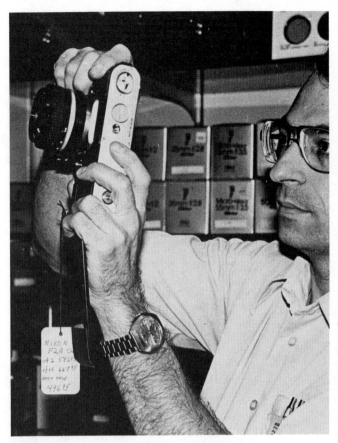

OPEN THE BACK of any camera you are considering, hold the unit to the light, and depress the shutter. Check to see that everything works smoothly and easily. Check the operation at different time settings.

■ LOOKING FOR A WAY to upgrade the quality of your photography equipment? A very good way to do it inexpensively is to buy used equipment—notably cameras. By shopping carefully, you can own the best camera of its type at a price you can afford.

The trick, of course, is in knowing how to judge the used camera you are buying. Here are some simple checks you can perform to help assure yourself of a good buy:

1. Know the kind of camera you want before you start to shop. Even make a decision as to the brand and model, if possible. Then visit several camera stores and make a cursory check. Is the camera you want available used? What is the price range? What is the general condition of the equipment?

This information should lead you to the dealer with the best stock and the best prices, and give you a "feel" of the market.

2. Select the most promising dealer and visit him to talk some serious business. Select the camera that seems to fit your situation both in price and in general condition. Now settle down with that camera and perform a thorough inspection.

3. First, the appearance. How does it look? Does it show signs of heavy wear? Look for dents and other clues that it may have been dropped. Look for signs of corrosion, and for evidence of an accumulation of dirt—anything that tells you the camera didn't receive good care. Check the tiny screws that hold it together. If they are burred, suspect that an amateur tried to repair it.

Reject the camera if you suspect it was dropped, was badly cared for, or repaired by an amateur. A well-worn camera can be a good camera—but only if it was cared for.

4. Check the serial number, and if it has been deleted, reject the camera. Is the interior clean, showing care? Snap the shutter and advance the film controls. Watch to see that all the controls function smoothly. Look to see that the shutter is absolutely undamaged.

5. Thread a roll of film into the camera to see that all the parts work smoothly. Most camera stores have an exposed roll you can use for this purpose. If not, bring your own, or even invest in a new roll. Remember, you are making a considerable investment.

6. Remove the lens, or, if the lens doesn't come off, open the back of the camera so you can look through it. Put the shutter on "bulb" and hold the lens toward the light. Look for nicks, scratches, discoloration or disfiguration. Ignore small air bubbles, since these appear in most lenses. While the lens is open, move the lens aperture to each of the f-stops. The iris blades should move in unison and form a symmetrical opening (usually hexagonal) at each stop, and each opening should be half (or double) the area of the one next to it.

WITH THE BACK of an SLR camera open, depress the shutter and observe the action of the focal plane shutter. Cock the camera and look again.

RUN A ROLL of exposed or out of date film through the camera, noting the action. All parts should work smoothly with no binding.

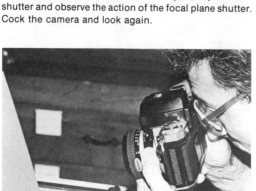

TEST A BUILT-IN METER by taking a reading from a Kodak gray card. Place the card in a light place and note the reading given by the meter.

NEXT, TAKE A READING with a good light meter, using the same gray card and placing the meter in the same position as the camera. Readings should agree.

7. Now, with the lens aperture wide open, close the shutter and run a similar test. With the camera toward the light, cock and fire the shutter at each of its speeds, up and down the scale. It should look and sound consistently faster or slower than the previous setting. If the blades on either the iris or the shutter stick—or in severe cases flop loose—reject the camera. On a camera with interchangeable lens, make the shutter and aperture tests separately.

If examining an interchangeable lens, see that the threads are undamaged. Shake it and listen for loose elements. Move the turning rings with your fingers to be sure they move easily but at the same time are snugly in place. Reject the lens if the rings are loose and wobbly.

8. Check the accessories. For example, fit a flash gun into the accessory shoe and fire the camera—to be sure that shoe contacts are good.

9. If the camera has a built-in exposure meter, check it by borrowing a Kodak gray card from the dealer (he has them in stock). Set the card up in a light place and look at it through the camera, taking a reading from the meter in the camera. Now borrow a good light meter (or bring your own) and make a reading, placing the meter at the same distance from the gray card as the camera was. The two readings should agree. Otherwise you can suspect trouble in the camera's built-in unit.

10. If the camera has a focal plane shutter (a flat cloth shutter which travels from one side to the other, visible when the back is off the camera) examine it to see that there are no holes. You can test it for timing and operation in the following manner: Borrow a small electronic flash unit. Place it on the counter, attached to the camera so that it will fire when you depress the shutter but-

REMOVE THE LENS from cameras with interchangeable lenses. Examine the lens threads or bayonet lugs and fittings for damage.

TEST SHUTTER by this test, using an electronic flash gun. Connect the gun to the camera, then place the gun so it fires directly into lens.

ton (use a short connector cord). With the back off the camera so you can see the shutter, place the camera so the flash gun fires directly into the lens. (See accompanying photos.) Place a small sheet of white paper over the shutter and set the time on the camera for flash synchronization, usually 1/60 of a second.

Now keep your eye on the white paper and depress the shutter button. The gun will fire and you should be able to see the entire rectangular shutter opening outlined on the paper. Now set the timer at 1/125-second and repeat. The size of the rectangle you see should be smaller. Make the test at 1/250. By now, when the flash fires, you should be able to see only a small part of the rectangle. At 1/500, you should see none of the rectangle.

This is a good test to indicate whether the shutter timing is functioning and is more or less accurate.

11. Check the focus by looking at objects through the camera. Bring them into sharp focus. Then measure with a tape the distance from the camera to the object. The footage scale on the lens should agree with your measurements.

If these seem like too many tests to perform in a camera store, ask the dealer for a trial period. Most will allow you 10 days. Take the camera home and make the tests at your leisure. Also shoot some test rolls and have them processed. During the tests it is best to use a tripod to assure steady pictures. Otherwise, you may blame the camera for fuzziness when actually it was your own body motion that caused the problem. Shoot some detailed subjects, such as a brick wall, from a distance of six feet. Make an enlargement of the

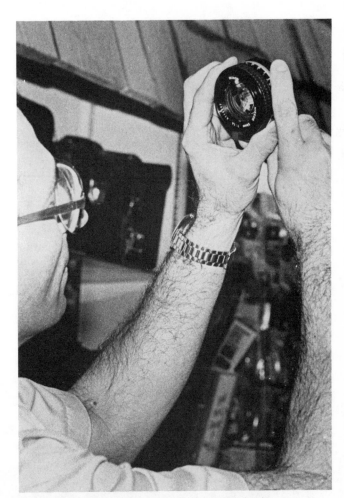

HOLD THE LENS up to the light and look through it. Look for scratches, discoloration and other damage. Ignore tiny bubbles, which are in many lenses. Shake the lens and listen for rattle.

WITH FLASH UNIT pointing into lens, place piece of paper over shutter. Set camera at 1/60-second, fire flash, and watch rectangle on paper.

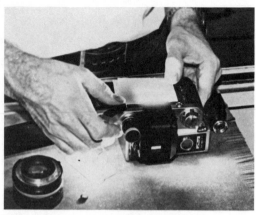

FULL rectangular opening of shutter should be visible at 1/60 during flash. About half is visible at 1/125, and a quarter at 1/250 of a second.

resulting picture and examine it for sharpness of detail. Shoot a sequence of pictures of the same subject, using all the f-stops and a series of different times. Compare these pictures. Look for a sharp fall off of focus from the center to the edges of the pictures. And look for a steady progression of exposures in the series of time pictures.

Ask the dealer about his guarantee. Most good dealers will allow 30 to 90 days on used equipment, depending on the conditions, brand and price asked.

If the camera is in top shape, don't expect too low a price. You should save a fair amount, depending on the age of the unit, but if the price is too low, be suspicious. The camera may have a history of repairs and the dealer may be trying to dump it.

In general, stay away from antiques—cameras more than 15 years old—unless you are a collector. It is also a good idea to avoid off brands when buying used equipment. Don't be surprised if you find some very recent models available in the used market. Often a shutterbug overextends himself for a new camera, then finds he must sell it back to the dealer to get some ready cash. Cameras acquired under these conditions will have very little use, but will be priced close to the new camera figure.

When looking at any camera, use your nose. Check to see if it has a smell of mildew, and look to see if there is evidence that the camera may have been water soaked. If you see any such signs, pass it by.

ADDING A Skylight (UV) filter to your lens will protect it from fingerprints and scratches. Such ultraviolet filters have no effect except to reduce the haze on distant shots, require no adjustment in exposure and can be left on a lens permanently.

Keep your camera shooting with these simple tips

■ EIGHTY PERCENT of all camera troubles are caused by dirt. Since dirt is a camera's No. 1 enemy, it follows that getting rid of it is the No. 1 step in good camera care. This is especially important when photo equipment has lain around unused for a time, as is often the case during the winter months. Fine dust particles can sift into a camera just sitting untouched on a shelf. Oily fingerprints and moisture attract and hold dirt like glue so that grimy deposits quickly build up.

If you just haul out your camera and start banging away with it, you grind the accumulated dirt deeper into the controls and delicate mechanisms. Your shutter starts to slow down, your flash synchronization goes out, the film advance may jam, and suddenly you're in trouble.

The most likely spots for dirt to seep into a camera are around the controls. These should be kept clean by regular brushing with a soft camel's-hair brush. Use a small, good-quality paintbrush or a photographer's lens brush. Built-up grime that can't be brushed away can be removed with a cotton swab dipped in rubbing alcohol. Also use a cotton swab and alcohol on the windows for viewfinders, range finders and built-in exposure meters.

Delicate parts like the lens, the film pressure plate and the mirror on reflex-type cameras re-

GLASS WINDOWS for viewfinders, range finders and exposure meters often become clouded with grime. Keep them clean with a cotton swab and alcohol to dissolve film deposits.

KEEP LENSES CLEAN with a soft brush. Use a special photographer's lens brush for this. The one shown above combines a bristle tip with a rubber syringe for blowing a stream of air, useful after brushing.

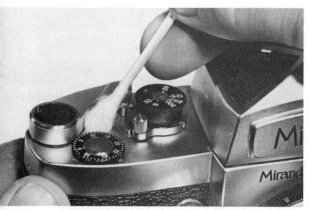

DIRT AND GRIME collect around a camera's controls and can eventually work their way inside, gumming up intricate mechanisms. Remove such deposits with a cotton swab dipped in rubbing alcohol.

A VACUUM CLEANER is handy for removing dust from hard-to-reach places in the camera. Use it only on suction, though; never when it's on blow. A blast of air can force dust particles deeper into critical parts or add new dirt, complicating the cleaning task.

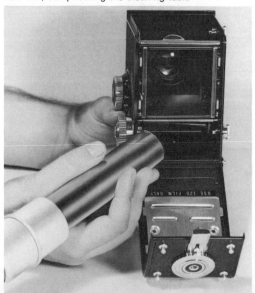

A DELICATE MIRROR used in a reflex-type camera requires special handling. You can brush it lightly if necessary, but it's even better to use only a gentle air stream from a syringe, as shown below.

BLOW DUST from inside the camera with a small rubber syringe. If the mirror is the type you can lock up, clean it first in the down position, then raise it out of the way and blow out the dirt behind it.

quire special care. The pressure plate is found on the inside of the camera back and its function is to keep the film flat and smooth behind the lens. You can brush gently around it, but be very careful not to scratch it. A scratch on the plate will, in turn, scratch the film pressed against it.

When working with lenses and mirrors, proceed with extreme caution. Use the least amount of cleaning that will do the job. Most people overclean their lenses while ignoring the rest of the camera. Excessive wiping can damage the thin antihalation coating on a lens and cause scratches. Start by blowing dust particles away with a small rubber syringe or special blower brush. These are available at camera shops and drugstores. Dirt that can't be blown away can be loosened by gentle brushing. On removable lenses, clean the rear element as well as the front one.

If necessary, the blowing and brushing can be followed by a light wiping with lens-cleaning tissue to remove any remaining film. Use only the special tissue made for this purpose, however—never a handkerchief or other cloth as the threads can cause scratches.

On mirrors, use only a combination of blowing and gentle brushing. Never touch or wipe a mirror or you may damage its precise alignment. Also never remove a lens and leave the opening in the camera exposed. Cover the hole with a body cap or keep a lens on the camera at all

Dirt inside a camera is even worse than on a lens. Open the back and shake the camera first to dislodge any bits of film or paper that may have been torn off around the sprockets. Then brush or blow out the interior with a can of pressurized air, being very careful around the pressure plate and the thin curtain on cameras with focal-plane shutters. Follow this with blowing to remove particles loosened by the brush. Always use a syringe for this. Never blow with your mouth, or moisture in your breath will collect in the camera and cause rusting.

A vacuum cleaner is handy for removing dust, but use it only on suction. If you blow with it, you'll blast more dirt into the camera than you take out. Be careful not to touch anything inside the camera with the metal nozzle. Never attempt to oil any of the mechanisms, either. This is a job for a professional.

After cleaning, the next thing to check on is your shutter. Shutter speeds generally slow down as dirt deposits build up. Run a test roll of film through the camera at different exposures. Try some shots with and without flash. The exposures that are indicated as correct for your test scenes should produce good results, and there should be an even gradation of light and dark pictures on either side of the correct exposure.

Also try a series of tests at the same exposure but using different combinations of shutter speeds and lens openings. Open up the lens a stop at a time as you use progressively faster speeds. If your shutter is working properly, all of your test results will be exactly the same since the exposures are identical. If they aren't, it's an indication that your timing is off.

If there are signs of trouble, take your camera to a professional repairman and ask to have the shutter adjusted. Don't attempt to do this job yourself.

TINY SCREWS in lens barrels and other camera parts frequently work loose and fall out, causing serious damage. Give them a periodic tightening with a small jeweler's or model-maker's screwdriver.

USE LIQUID LENS cleaner only as a last resort to remove stubborn gummy deposits. Swab it on gently with a wadded-up lens-cleaning tissue, then wipe the lens dry. Excessive use of liquid cleaner can harm a len's coating.

A SOFT-BRISTLE paintbrush of the narrow sash and trim type is useful for getting into crevices inside a camera. Brush out the film compartment, but don't damage the fabric curtain on cameras with focal-plane shutters.

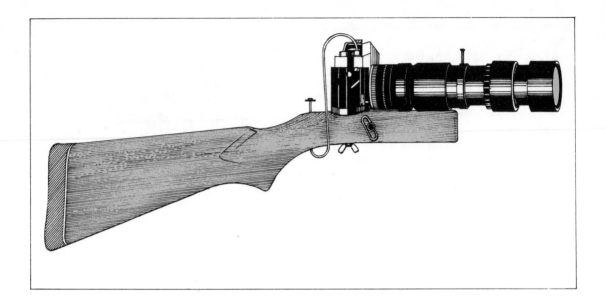

Inexpensive telephoto gunstock

■ ARE YOUR TELEPHOTO shots blurry? A gunstock will steady your camera without tying it down as a tripod would. And though commercial camera stocks are relatively expensive, you can build one easily and inexpensively.

Start with a used or unfinished gunstock. Check its size by taping your camera in place and holding it. You can cut down the stock (after allowing for thickness of the butt plate) or add a thicker butt plate as needed.

The camera mounts with a bolt through the stock's trigger slot. Cut a ¼-inch metal plate a bit longer and wider than the slot and drill a ⁵/₁₆-inch hole in it for the camera bolt (you can try a large, heavy washer if no means are handy for cutting metal).

If you can find a ¼-20 thumbscrew long enough to reach the camera through the slot, use

it. Otherwise, force-fit, braze or epoxy a wingnut to the head of a ¼-20 bolt. Start with a bolt a trifle long, then grind it back, a bit at a time, until it just holds the camera snugly by its tripod socket.

Drill a hole down through the stock for a cable release. You can run the release up from under the stock, but you may find it more convenient to press it from the top with your thumb. Now all that's left to do is to finish or refinish the stock. You can also add sling swivels, if you like.

SCREW AND mounting plate, inserted from under the stock, hold the camera by its tripod hole.

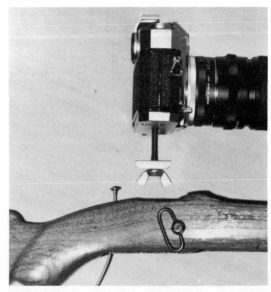

INDEX · VOLUME 4

PIPE FITTINGS

NIPPLES

PIPE LENGTHS UP TO 22 FT.

STRAIGHT COUPLING

REDUCING COUPLING

COUPLING

NUT

CAP

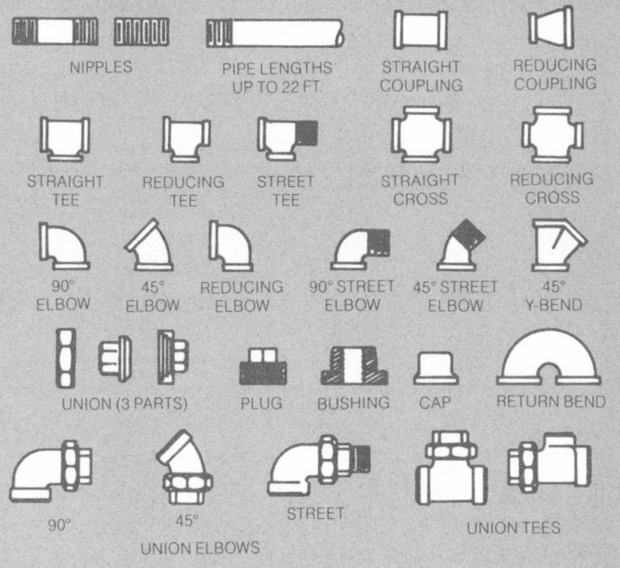

STRAIGHT TEE   REDUCING TEE   STREET TEE   STRAIGHT CROSS   REDUCING CROSS

90° ELBOW

90° ELBOW

90° ELBOW   45° ELBOW   REDUCING ELBOW   90° STREET ELBOW   45° STREET ELBOW   45° Y-BEND

REDUCING TEE

REDUCER

UNION (3 PARTS)   PLUG   BUSHING   CAP   RETURN BEND

90°

45°

STREET

UNION ELBOWS

UNION TEES

PLUG

45° ELBOW

TEE

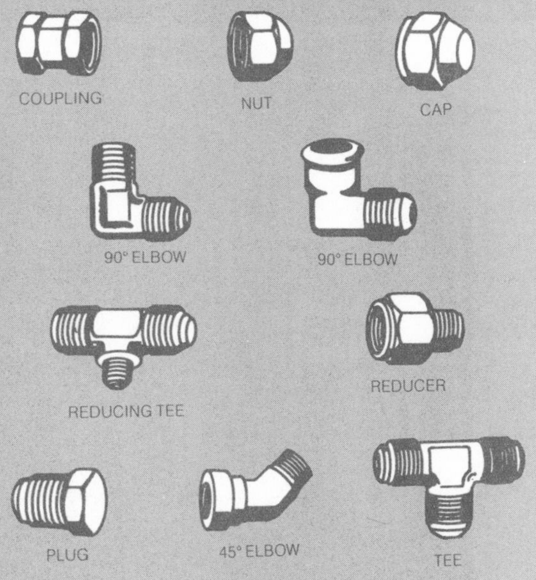

MEASURES OF CAPACITY

1 cup	=	8 fl oz
2 cups	=	1 pint
2 pints	=	1 quart
4 quarts	=	1 gallon
2 gallons	=	1 peck
4 pecks	=	1 bushel

STANDARD STEEL PIPE ((All Dimensions in inches)					
Nominal Size	Outside Diameter	Inside Diameter	Nominal Size	Outside Diameter	Inside Diameter
⅛	0.405	0.269	1	1.315	1.049
¼	0.540	0.364	1¼	1.660	1.380
⅜	0.675	0.493	1½	1.900	1.610
½	0.840	0.622	2	2.375	2.067
¾	1.050	0.824	2½	2.875	2.469

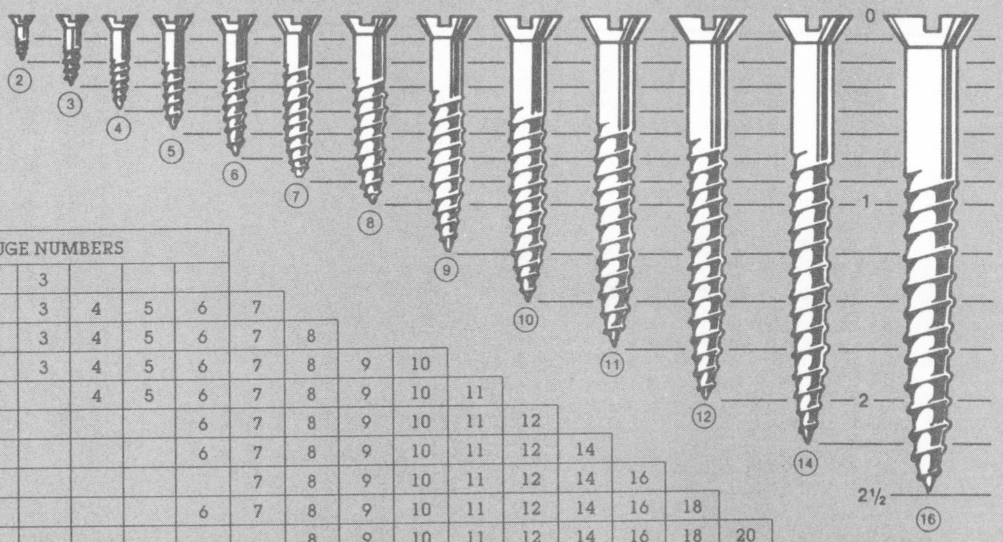

WOOD SCREWS

LENGTH	GAUGE NUMBERS														
¼ INCH	0	1	2	3											
⅜ INCH			2	3	4	5	6	7							
½ INCH			2	3	4	5	6	7	8						
⅝ INCH				3	4	5	6	7	8	9	10				
¾ INCH					4	5	6	7	8	9	10	11			
⅞ INCH							6	7	8	9	10	11	12		
1 INCH							6	7	8	9	10	11	12	14	
1¼ INCH								7	8	9	10	11	12	14	16
1½ INCH							6	7	8	9	10	11	12	14	16	18
1¾ INCH									8	9	10	11	12	14	16	18	20
2 INCH									8	9	10	11	12	14	16	18	20
2¼ INCH										9	10	11	12	14	16	18	20
2½ INCH													12	14	16	18	20
2¾ INCH														14	16	18	20
3 INCH															16	18	20
3½ INCH																18	20	24
4 INCH																18	20	24

WHEN YOU BUY SCREWS, SPECIFY (1) LENGTH, (2) GAUGE NUMBER, (3) TYPE OF HEAD—FLAT, ROUND, OR OVAL, (4) MATERIAL—STEEL, BRASS, BRONZE, ETC., (5) FINISH—BRIGHT, STEEL BLUED, CADMIUM, NICKEL, OR CHROMIUM PLATED.